Secrets from the Flower Farm

Growing
abundant flowers
in unpredictable
conditions

Rebecca Starling & Christine McCabe
Photography by Christopher Morrison

T&H

Contents

Introduction 7

Secrets from the Flower Farm

Have you ever wondered how some gardeners manage to grow armfuls of incredible flowers in gorgeous colours for months on end? Do photos of romantic gardens stuffed with wispy cosmos or dahlias the size of dinner plates seem the preserve of magazines? How is this achievable in a small garden, even a balcony? What is the secret to growing abundant, fragrant and achingly fashionable cut flowers?

Secrets from the Flower Farm examines different, sometimes unexpected, ways of growing; adapts age-old gardening advice for tricky conditions; and discusses tough, surprising plant choices that will provide cut flowers for up to 12 months of the year. The Flower Farm lies in remote South Australia, a dry place with poor soils and unrelenting winds, yet it produces bountiful cut flowers using natural growing methods across all four seasons.

The Flower Farm was established 6 years ago by Rebecca Starling, a well-travelled gardener, flower farmer and London-trained florist, on her husband's family property. Christine McCabe is a travel writer and author who has nurtured a historic garden in the Adelaide Hills for 25 years. They met by chance in Rebecca's flower shop in the pretty seaside town of Robe, got chatting and discovered a shared love of flowers and gardening. Very quickly they decided to co-host workshops detailing the ins and outs of growing cut flowers, introducing people to many varieties unknown or long since forgotten. Participants were so engaged, so eager to learn more and so besotted with Rebecca's beautiful flowers, the idea of writing this book and sharing the secrets of flower growing took hold.

The gradual cultivating of 'secrets' and growing tips that would lead to this wonderfully productive Flower Farm had its genesis on the other side of the world. Rebecca began her gardening life in an English village, before upping garden stakes and moving to the Swiss Alps. Following this high-altitude gardening adventure, she spent several years grappling with extremely cold winters in leafy Connecticut in the USA (USDA zone 6b*), before finally alighting in sunny Australia.

Each of these four places had different growing conditions with little in common. Growing techniques that worked in one location totally failed in the next. Even so, patterns and common threads began to emerge, and, over the years, Rebecca developed an adaptive method of growing that was further refined at the Flower Farm as she embarked on the search for the perfect cut flower.

Each season, the flowers went through a rigorous review. Did they grow well, with little pest, sun and wind damage? Did the colours engage and excite customers? Were all viable stems used, or did some go to waste? Any flower that didn't make the grade was discontinued the following year. And learning the secret to a great bouquet – a mix of flower shapes and sizes in seasonally suitable colours – meant growing flowers that worked together in harmony. This allowed growing space to be allocated to a mix of plants that would yield buckets of beautiful flowers time and time again.

In these pages you'll learn how to plan a cutting garden and grow beautiful flowers, wherever in the world you are. Your conditions will be different to those of the Flower Farm, so expect a process of trial and error as you uncover what works best where you live. This book will help shortcut that journey and suggest alternatives if Plan A doesn't pan out.

If you've had garden failures in the past (and honestly, who hasn't!), it's quite possible that the growing advice you followed was better suited to a different part of the world. This is a particular challenge for southern hemisphere growers; many gardening books are written for the northern hemisphere, assuming gardens with snowy winters, long springs, temperate summers, and autumns punctuated by frosts. For warm-climate growers, we share fresh approaches (and time-saving hacks) to help grow abundant flowers.

Weather everywhere is becoming less predictable and can differ markedly from year to year. Many places are experiencing hotter, drier summers, while others are struggling to manage torrential rain and flooding. There are lessons to be learnt from gardeners in other parts of the world. We share some of these lessons and shine a light on beautiful cut flowers from hot, dry places: Australian and South African native plants, fragrant Mediterranean shrubs, and perennials from the North American prairies.

*The USDA Plant Hardiness Zone Map divides the US into eleven geographic zones based on the average minimum winter temperatures. The map is used to give gardeners an indication as to which plants are most likely to survive over winter where they live. Similar plant hardiness zone maps exist for other countries.

A vibrant cutting garden is possible wherever you live – one that is both manageable and productive. To start growing, all you need is a handful of pots on an apartment balcony or a single raised bed – the size of a dining table – in a small garden or courtyard. The benefits are incredible. Fresher flowers, wondrous fragrance, zero air miles and much more variety, with countless drop-dead-gorgeous flowers that you won't find in a florist.

And never underestimate the enjoyment and incredible satisfaction that can be yours by simply popping a few bulbs in a pretty container and waiting for spring.

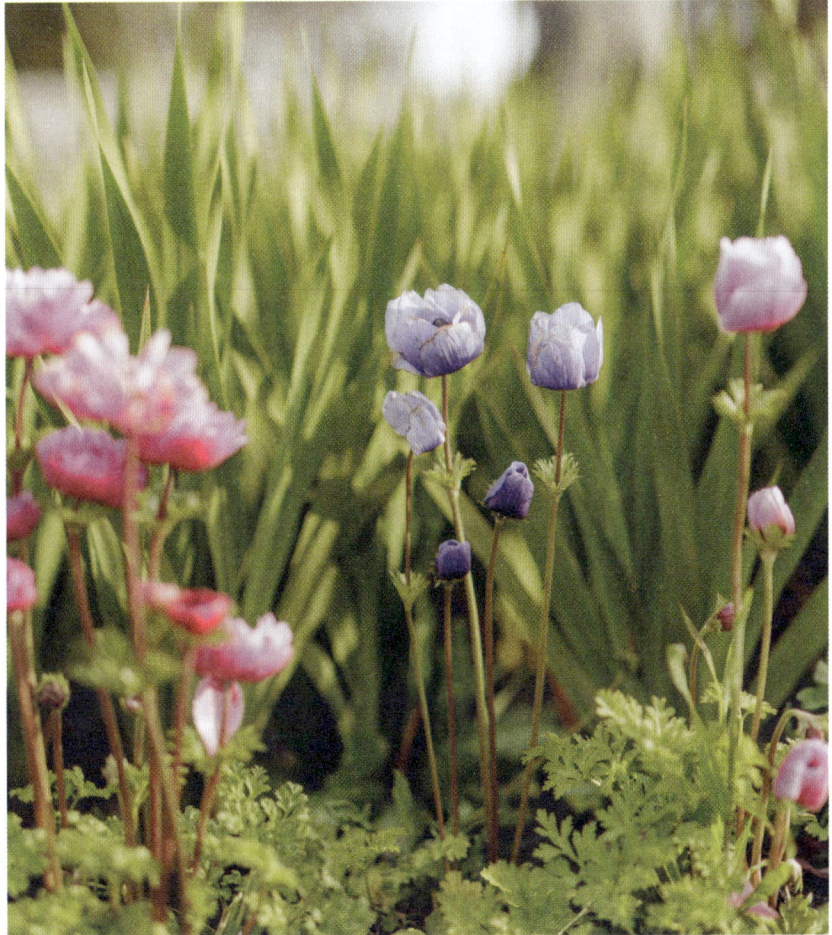

PREVIOUS PAGE Cafe au lait dahlias.

TOP Early summer morning on the Flower Farm with dahlias ready for cutting.

RIGHT Anemones are one of the joys of spring. They are equally happy planted in garden beds or pots.

Creating your

cutting garden.

Wherever you live you can grow cut flowers. The secret lies in selecting plants that are happy in your garden and will thrive in the prevailing conditions. In this chapter we discuss the elements you'll need to consider when establishing a cutting garden. Many cut flowers grow best in:

- An open site in full sun

- Well-drained loamy soil, high in organic matter

- A site protected from the wind

- Soil pH slightly acid to neutral (pH 6–7)

- Fresh, low-salinity water.

Few of us will be able to tick every box on this list but that's fine. There are cut flowers for every situation and ways to help a garden become more resilient. Do not be deterred if your gardening conditions seem less than perfect.

Your Garden's Conditions

'Right Plant Right Place' is a catchphrase coined in the 1960s by the widely admired English garden writer and plantswoman Beth Chatto. Cleverly chosen plants need fewer resources (water, fertiliser and work) and are less likely to suffer from pests and disease. 'Right Plant Right Place' is especially important when growing cut flowers. The role of the cutting garden is to supply perfect flowers atop long, strong stems with maximum vase life. Plants struggling in unsuitable conditions will have smaller flowers on shorter, weaker stems with a reduced vase life. Fortunately, there is a huge variety of plants that make excellent cut flowers; you will find plenty to suit your conditions without compromising on design.

PREVIOUS PAGE Joyful spring flowers in the studio, ready to be arranged.

LEFT Watsonia 'Lilac Towers' is a popular addition to our spring bunches.

RIGHT Metallic-blue sea holly needs little water once established.

Understanding your garden

Even a small garden or cutting patch will have warmer and cooler areas, sheltered spots and windy corridors, dry patches, and rich, moist corners. On larger plots, widely variant microclimates are common, and your garden will not have precisely the same growing conditions as your neighbour's. A wall or tall hedge may create a dry, shady spot in an otherwise bright, sunny garden. A windy, exposed plot may be protected in parts by a house or other building. If your garden is not flat, you might notice that cool air becomes trapped at the bottom of the slope in winter, creating a frost pocket and an area less suited to tender plants. Before planning your cutting garden and ordering seeds and plants, grab a notebook and record the conditions you observe in your garden:

- **Orientation, prevailing weather and wind direction.** Check the prevailing wind direction and track changes at various times of the year, temperature (summer highs and winter lows), rain (when and how much), humidity, seasonal storms, frost start and end dates. Observe the orientation of your garden at various times of the day to see which parts are in sun and shade and note how that alters through the seasons. Invest in a rain gauge and keep a record of rainfall amounts across the year.

- **Soil.** Is it sandy, clay or loam? Does the soil drain well or does water lie on the ground for a long period after rain? How fertile is the soil and what is the pH (acid, neutral or alkaline)? pH soil testing kits and pH meters are widely available.

- **History.** A new-build house often has a thin layer of topsoil covering sand and builders' rubble. An established garden that has received plenty of compost love over the years will have richer, more fertile soil. These gardens will provide different conditions and suit different plants.

With a better understanding of your garden's conditions, it's easier to select plants that will thrive. It can be helpful to keep some key words in mind. Gardening books, websites and seed packets tend to use similar language. Are you looking for plants that are *drought-tolerant* or *low water* that thrive in *well-drained soil* in *full sun*? Or is your perfect match more suited to *heavy clay* or *part shade*?

Local information is also critical. Check the websites of local botanical gardens, good plant nurseries and independent garden centres in your area. They'll be able to recommend plants that will thrive in your garden and what to avoid. If you're plant shopping online, many specialist plant websites have filters that allow you to select for cut flowers, growing conditions and soil type.

ABOVE Rain can be localised, so we installed a Flower Farm rain gauge to keep track.

RIGHT Jerusalem artichokes make a pretty autumn cut flower.

Planning for unpredictable weather

In matching plant to place you are making your best assessment, through observation and research, of the growing conditions in your garden both now and into the future. However, as gardeners and flower farmers across the world know only too well, this is not a precise science and one year can differ markedly from the next. In recent years the unpredictability of our climate has amped up with rain bombs, heatwaves, forest fires, floods, storms and droughts keeping us on our toes. But there's plenty you can do to improve your garden's resilience:

- **Create windbreaks for storm protection.** If your garden is exposed to possibly damaging winds – and it doesn't take a lot to flatten tall flower spikes – you'll need to establish wind breaks or barriers. On the Flower Farm, Australian and South African native trees and shrubs create a flowering windbreak, useful and pretty in equal measure.

- **Mulch or add compost to retain water.** As well as feeding plants and improving the soil, a layer of compost or mulch reduces water requirements while helping plants to establish strong root systems. A strong root system improves a plant's ability to cope with hot summer temperatures.

- **Improve drainage to deal with deluges.** If your soil drains poorly or your garden suffers from seasonal floods, consider building raised beds or digging drainage trenches alongside flower beds, directing the saved water to a pond.

- **Capture rainwater.** Rainwater harvesting is one step we can take to help our flowers survive a dry summer. In urban areas garden run-off entering storm-water systems, along with soil erosion, is lessened if water is captured on site. Tank size and design is improving, with small oblong versions perfect for tucking against the wall of your home.

Windbreaks

These fast-growing windbreaks also look great in the vase.

- Jerusalem artichokes. *Lovely small sunflower blooms and tasty tubers for the kitchen.*

- Sunflowers. *Gorgeous large flowers; seed for overwintering birds.*

- Sweetcorn. *Delicious; also charming in dried arrangements.*

- Canna lilies. *For dramatic leaves wrapped around the inside of a glass vase.*

- Tree dahlias. *Stake these tall plants.*

- Clematis, sweet peas and hyacinth bean. *Grow as vines on an arbour.*

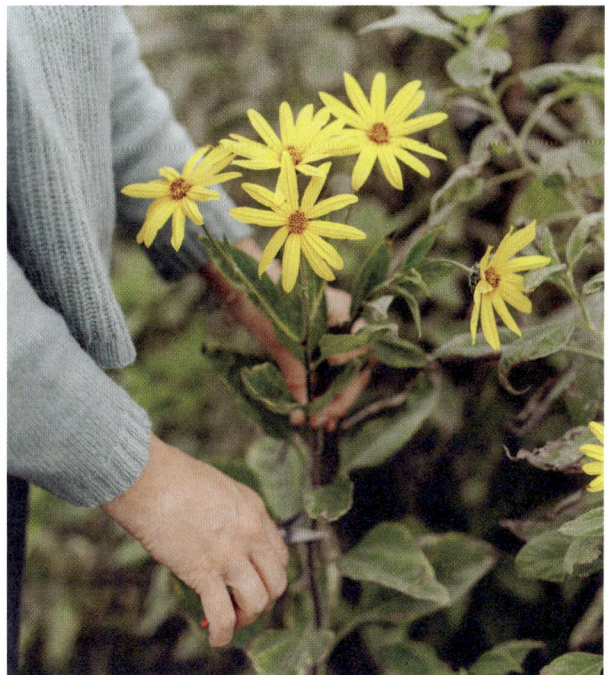

Adjusting how you grow

In planning your cutting garden, it can help to research what works for growers in other climate zones and how they manage challenging conditions. In hot countries, it's routine to prepare for the fire season by removing leaf litter, reducing the vegetive fuel load and clearing fire breaks. In some parts of the world water tanks are common, even in urban areas, and people manage the impact of drought by harvesting their own rainwater. Similarly, look to cooler places for practical ways to manage the impact of surprise frosts. Lightweight row covers can quickly be used to cover tender plants if the weather forecast reveals cooler overnight temperatures than you had expected.

The growing methods outlined in this book are based on lessons picked up while growing flowers in markedly different conditions around the world. These include sowing seed or planting at different times in the year, choosing tougher plants or looking to other parts of the world for different ways of growing:

- If your spring and summer months are becoming wetter and your soil is not well drained, plant rot-prone plants such as dahlias, ranunculus or sea holly in raised beds where plants are away from sitting ground water.

- If your spring is becoming warmer and you're struggling to get seedlings established before they fry under a hot sun, try sowing your cold-hardy annual seeds in early autumn while the ground is still warm. This allows the plants to put down strong roots before winter when the ground cools. You'll be amazed at how many different varieties of cut flowers can be grown, even in cold places, using this method..If sufficiently hardy, the seedlings will survive the winter, bounce into growth in early spring and be better able to withstand the spring and summer sun.

- If summers in your region are becoming hotter and drier, look to warm, dry places to see which plants thrive. Australian, South African, Mediterranean and North American prairie plants are a good place to start. Many are water wise and drought resistant once established. Also look at growing methods in those countries. Shade cloth may be more useful than frost protection, while mulch is applied in summer to retain moisture and shade roots rather than protect borderline hardy plants in winter.

RIGHT A block of tightly planted sunflowers acts as a windbreak for beds of zinnias. The seed heads are left to feed overwintering birds.

Drought-tolerant favourites

Perfect for a dry spot in your cutting garden.

- *Eryngium planum* 'Blue Glitter'. A silver-blue sea holly growing about 1 metre tall. Grown from seed, it will flower in the first season after planting. Once established it will flower several weeks earlier than other varieties.

- *Eryngium giganteum* 'Miss Willmott's Ghost'. This hardy sea holly glows at dusk with a silvery white sheen, hence the spooky name. Pretty in the garden as well as in bunches.

- *Echinacea purpurea* 'White Swan'. Fresh, modern and smelling enticingly of honey. Loved by bees.

- Kangaroo paw (*Anigozanthos*). Taller varieties are the easiest to grow and longest surviving plants. Drought-tolerant once established.

- Obedient plant (*Physostegia virginiana*). So called because the petals can be moved around the stem where they stay put. This plant tolerates all conditions from dry to waterlogged. A great cut flower but keep it in check as is does like to spread. Fortunately, the shallow rooted stems are easy to pull out.

- *Salvia leucantha*. This hardy salvia is great for cutting. Lovely arching purple or white flowers last late into winter (or until the first hard frost in cooler climates). Survives with no irrigation but the stems are longer with a little water.

LEFT Excess sea holly is useful for drying.

BELOW 'Blue Bedder' salvia is our favourite salvia to pair with roses.

RIGHT Cut kangaroo paw above a side shoot for multiple flowers and a long flowering window.

A Flower-filled Home

Grow what you love

Once you have assessed your garden's growing conditions, draw up a wish list of the flowers you want to see in your home. Scour gardening books and online seed catalogues, spend lazy mornings in the plant nursery or dip into the podcasts of flower farmers and florists. This is such a fun part of the process and one of the favourite jobs on the Flower Farm – planning and dreaming.

Whatever you grow, make sure it's a flower you really love, providing the Right Plant Right Place rule fits of course. Your cutting garden should be a place of joy, somewhere to retreat, to forget work and daily chores for a while. Consider which flowers will best complement your home, whether that is cooling whites and greens in a modern space or bright neon colours to add seasonal variety to a monochrome scheme. Cottage garden flowers are right at home in little, low-ceilinged spaces whereas you might prefer blooms with richer, luxurious tones to adorn a formal dining room.

If you have a larger garden and are not renting, consider investing in permanent shrubs and trees and favourites like peonies and roses. These are always useful for cutting and will stand the test of fashion time. Quick-grow, economical annuals are the perfect fast-fashion solution. Swap them out every year for new colours and styles.

When making a wish list, remember that fashion influences flowers as powerfully as it does the clothes we wear. Flowers and flower shapes fall in and out of fashion. Dahlias, gladioli, gypsophila – on trend or very last year? Social media is ensuring trends are swapped in and out with increasing speed. Faster than the flowers can grow!

These Flower Farm secrets can help you manage flower fashion so you love what you grow:

- Be authentic. Lean into your personal style and cultivate that. We love the classic cottage garden look – wild, organic, loosely bound bunches of scented, whimsical flowers. You might prefer something very different.

- Look to fashion week. What colours dominate the catwalks and are they becoming brighter, softer, muddier or more neon?

- Check out interior design trends. How do flowers fit popular colour palettes and moods? Is the style moving towards minimalism, maximalism, organic and natural or sleek and urban?

- Be counterintuitive. People often have a strong aversion to a colour or style just before it swings back into fashion.

- Look overseas. What are florists, flower farmers and gardeners using on the other side of the world?

- Wider trends. Are other factors impacting flower growing? Sustainability has become an important consideration.

LEFT Many happy hours can be spent planning colour schemes and discovering new cut flower candidates.

Suit the season

When ordering seeds and plants, consider a colour scheme to suit the season. Firm favourites at the Flower Farm are:

Spring

Candy Store Pastels

Spring bulbs are perfect for Easter in the northern hemisphere. Tulips in a mix of white and pastel tones are a delight. In the southern hemisphere, Easter falls in early autumn. Snapdragons, pastel achillea and pompon dahlias in pinks and whites provide similar candy tones. Other spring combinations include monochromatic pinks and reds or clashing primary colours.

RIGHT A pretty Easter egg hunt decorated with green tomatillo lanterns, 'Appleblossom' snapdragons and chocolate eggs galore.

Summer

Clean and Fresh

White shines in summer. Enjoy crisp, clean tones with the zingy freshness of new leaves and stems as contrast. Other summer combinations include beachy blues, yellows and whites, and bright mixed bunches.

Autumn

Sunset Tones

Amplify autumn's golden tones by pulling together a glowing bunch of peach, apricot, mustard and rust tones. Dahlias and the North American prairie plants evoke a sunburnt landscape. Other autumn combinations include texture-rich arrangements or mixed fresh and dry bunches.

Winter

Rich and Luxurious

Warm reds, deep purples and hot pinks are great for a winter dinner party, especially if lit with candlelight. Be sure to include some lighter tones so the flowers don't appear too dark. White can be jarring, so use dusky hues instead to create highlights. Think bicolour ornamental kale, scented stocks, red leucadendron and bronze wallflowers. Other winter combinations include cool purples and lilacs, quiet tones such as buttery lemon, apricot, soft pink and winter whites.

RIGHT White roses, Canterbury bells, ornithogalum and baby's breath in a long and low arrangement for a formal summer dinner.

Supplement your bouquet

If your cutting patch looks a little light, it's fine to plump out bouquets with shop-bought extras. Where possible, buy locally grown, seasonal flowers for a more sustainable alternative. If you don't have a garden or are gifted a bunch of flowers, these tips can help personalise a shop-bought bouquet.

- Mix in some foliage or airy elements, whether cut from your garden or foraged.

- Carefully take apart the bouquet and lay the stems on a table. Remake the bouquet to your liking, perhaps with additions, rearranging in your hand or a vase.

- In the case of big bouquets, split the stems among several little vases and enjoy flowers in multiple rooms in your home or cluster the vases as an installation on a table.

- If you have saved some dried flowers, these can be added for that personal touch.

Colour Theory

Even flower farmers can be swept off course by new flower shades and colours or exciting plant discoveries. When planning next season's cutting patch it's sometimes tempting to order absolutely everything.

Having a few 'go-to' colour combinations is a helpful shortcut when you're stuck for inspiration or in a rush. Find combinations that look good in your home and complement your aesthetic. The most beautiful bouquets and arrangements include flower colours that work well together. Here, the colour wheel can be a useful guide.

Monochrome Colours

Start by experimenting with different shades and tones of the same colour. Working with various shades of one colour makes it easier to create a cohesive arrangement. Add interest by playing around with different textures, shapes and sizes of flowers. Successful monochromatic floral designs include:

- **Soft pinks, hot pinks and reds**

- **Sunset tones of orange, peach and apricot**

- **Mustard, canary yellow and lemon**
  (make sure you have lots of whites and good foliage to soften this sunny bunch).

Analogous Colours

These sit next to each other on the colour wheel and make for a harmonious design. There are two groups:

- **Warm (red, orange, yellow)**

A warm scheme might feature a flower-heavy vase of dahlias, paper daisies and echinacea in deep red, fiery orange, and watermelon shades. Stripped of foliage, as green cools the colour scheme, this is a celebratory bunch for hot summer and autumn days.

- **Cool (blue, green, purple)**

A sample cool scheme might include a fresh, lush bunch of foliage: blue-grey eucalyptus or olive leaves, deep-green pittosporum or ruscus. Add some stems of lavender, delphinium, salvia, sea holly, white dahlias and feverfew for a soothing arrangement.

In both warm and cool designs, it's sometimes fun to add a pop of complementary colour, lending energy and excitement to a cool scheme or calming the intensity of a warm-toned bunch.

Complementary Colours

These sit opposite each other on the colour wheel and, put together, intensify each other – lifting vibrancy. Pairings include:

- **Yellow and purple**
- **Orange and blue**
- **Green and magenta**

When used as the principal colours in an arrangement, bold pairings can be challenging, slightly reminiscent of old-school floristry. A more modern take is to lighten the colours into their pastel forms. Peach and lilac are a favourite combination and, with planning, available in every season on the Flower Farm:

- Salmon Italian ranunculus and 'Misty Lavender' larkspur in spring
- Lavender-coloured 'Novalis' roses with 'Touch of Red Buff' calendula in summer
- Heirloom chrysanthemums in a mix of apricot, peach, lavender and light pink shades in autumn
- Apricot-scented stocks and 'Bowles's Mauve' perennial wallflower in winter.

Starting Your Cutting Garden

There's something rewarding and pleasurable about cutting a flower you have grown from seed. There's more work involved than buying seedlings or pots from the nursery, but if your goal is a vibrant cutting garden that produces amazing flowers in wonderful colours and forms, then growing from seed is essential. Although garden centres often sell plants such as celosia and lisianthus, these are typically dwarf bedding cultivars with stems too short for the vase. And you will rarely find the wonderful colours and forms featured in this book.

Packets of seed are inexpensive and can be stored for some time in a sealed jar in a cool, dry place, even in the fridge. Always sow more than you need, as no grower achieves a 100 per cent germination rate. If you're new to growing from seed, start with annuals (plants that complete their growth cycle within a year) as these are the fastest to germinate and easiest to grow. There are two key factors to consider:

- **When to sow.** This will depend on your conditions.

- **How to grow.** Direct-sow the seed into the ground or sow under cover in a greenhouse or on a sunny windowsill.

Take care when handling all seed but particularly sweet peas, delphiniums, larkspur and foxgloves, as the seed and plant parts are toxic.

TOP LEFT AND TOP RIGHT Newly planted seedlings are watered with a sprinkler to ensure the top layer of soil remains moist.

BOTTOM LEFT The many colours of heat-loving celosia.

BELOW Biennial Canterbury bells.

Annual, biennial, perennial

Perennials. Permanent or long-lasting trees and shrubs. Roses, peonies and most Australian and South African native plants are perennial. Within this group, some are deciduous and others evergreen.

Annuals. Complete an entire growing cycle within a year, germinating from seed, growing leaves, flowering, setting seed and dying. Easy to grow from seed. Described as hardy, half-hardy and tender depending on how well these plants tolerate cold weather.

Biennials. Complete a full life cycle in two growing seasons. In the first, roots, stems and leaves are produced. In the second, the plant turns its attention to flowers, fruit and seeds. Biennials planted in late summer can complete their first cycle in autumn and will commence their second cycle (and flower) during the following spring-summer.

Cold climates

Most advice in books, on seed packets and plant websites focuses on late winter or early spring sowing for northern hemisphere gardens with cold winters and heavy frosts. Here, the recommendation is to sow seeds under cover in the weeks prior to the last frost date (LFD). Once germinated, the seedlings are grown in a bright, frost-free place and planted outside once the LFD has passed. Depending on the hardiness of the plant, this might be immediately after the LFD or several weeks later for more tender varieties requiring warmer conditions.

Use the LFD for your location to calculate when to sow seeds. The lead time varies according to how quickly plants grow and is often stated on the seed packet. For example:

- Amaranthus is sown 4 to 6 weeks before the LFD.

- Gomphrena is sown 6 to 8 weeks before the LFD.

- Lisianthus is sown 12 weeks before the LFD.

As regions with cold winters often have shorter growing seasons, sowing under cover and then planting out established seedlings gives gardeners a head start, and, hopefully, more weeks of flowers before the arrival of autumn frosts. Ideally, seedlings should be mature enough to be planted out, but not so large they are root-bound in their containers.

Cold-hardy annuals

Cold-hardy annuals can survive cold winter temperatures, and many tough varieties can be sown in autumn. In USDA 7 or warmer climates they should survive in well-drained ground over winter but will need additional protection such as frost cloth or caterpillar tunnels during cold snaps or below USDA 7.

- Cornflowers*
- Scabiosa
- Snapdragons
- Sweet peas*
- Stock
- Clary sage
- Iceland poppies
- Love-in-a-mist*

- Bells of Ireland
- Calendula
- Larkspur*
- Feverfew*
- Queen Anne's lace or ammi
- Chinese forget-me-not
- Orlaya*

*These are some of the hardiest cold-hardy annuals.

ABOVE Calendula provides valuable winter colour in warm climates (from late spring in cooler places).

Warm climates

In warmer climates and places that are becoming warmer, there are different challenges when growing from seed. A powerful spring-summer sun can fry emergent seedlings in half an afternoon, and even on milder days the top layer of soil can be quickly dried out by a strong wind.

It's often easier to sow seed in autumn when the sun is lower in the sky and autumn rains are regular. Sow seeds once temperatures have dropped but before the ground has cooled. If your region is prone to frosts, count back from the 'first frost date' (FFD) to ensure any plants you're growing under cover are in the ground for at least a few weeks before this date.

The delicate balance between heat, rainfall and soil temperature will vary from place to place and year to year. Sow seed sooner if autumn looks to be arriving early; wait a couple of weeks if the weather remains hot and dry. Wriggle your fingers into the soil – warm and damp is perfect for planting.

If you're unsure which approach is right for you, sow a batch in autumn and plant into warm soil. If the plants don't make it through winter, you can always re-sow in late winter or early spring and plant out after the danger of frost has passed.

Remember that autumn-sown plants often stall over winter and put on little additional growth. But under the ground they will be establishing strong root systems ready to bounce into life in spring.

RIGHT Easy-to-grow feverfew is a great cut flower and a valuable bouquet filler.

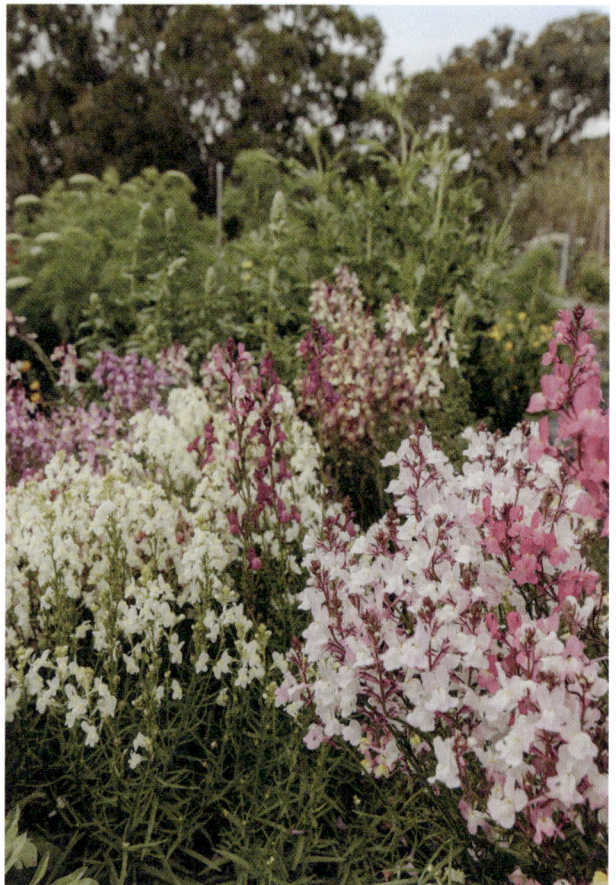

Where to sow

While it's tempting to scatter seed directly into the garden, as suggested on many seed packets, this can greatly diminish germination rates. Tiny seedlings are delicious to a wide variety of pests and can readily dry out before they've established a good root system. Pests can be kept at bay and moisture levels more easily regulated when seeds are grown under cover, and germination rates will increase. However, there are exceptions:

- Sunflowers and zinnias have large, carbohydrate-packed seeds. These germinate quickly and grow vigorously making them more able to tolerate pest damage and quickly put down roots. Easy and quick to grow, they are incredibly satisfying for the novice cut flower grower.

- Plants that hate having their roots disturbed when transferred from a seed tray into the ground, such as phlox or chocolate lace flower (*Daucus carota* 'Dara'), are best sown directly into the ground.

- Some plants need a period of winter cold to break dormancy and germinate (known as cold stratification), ready to start growing in spring.

Tip: *If you live in a warm place without winter frosts, cold stratify your seeds in the fridge for a few weeks before sowing.*

Sowing seed under cover

This process of sowing seed into small containers and growing the seedlings in a protected place until they're large enough to be planted in the ground is either referred to as sowing seed under cover or raising seedlings. It's the best method to ensure you achieve a full and vibrant cutting garden.

Seed can be sown into a wide variety of pots and containers. There must be holes in the bottom for drainage, and terracotta pots help regulate temperature and moisture levels but there's no need to buy new. Repurpose or recycle whatever is to hand. It's a great way of re-using unwanted food containers or giving plastic pots a second life. Fill your container with seed starting mix and start with an easy-to-grow variety. Keep the potting mix moist but not waterlogged, and in a week or two seedlings should magically emerge. They require plenty of light otherwise risk becoming 'leggy' chasing the sun, so experiment to find the perfect spot. Favourite easy growers include:

- Sweet peas
- Wallflowers
- Cosmos
- Strawflower/paper daisy
- Statice
- Gomphrena.

CLOCKWISE FROM TOP LEFT
Large sweet pea seeds are easy to collect and store; Sweet William has an incredibly long vase life; Incredible linaria resemble miniature snapdragons and make great cut flowers; Scented wallflowers are tough and incredibly drought-tolerant.

Cut and come again

'Cut and come again' (CCA) varieties are popular with flower farmers. The more you cut, the more replacement flowers will grow. Cosmos, zinnia, branching sunflower, dahlia and ranunculus are some of the best CCA flowers. A single plant can provide countless vases of flowers.

Succession sowing

Eventually, these amazing CCA varieties tire, flowers become smaller and stems shorter. By sowing multiple batches of seeds, staggered over a few weeks, you can dramatically extend the flowering season. Quick-grow CCA flowers are especially good for succession sowing.

- Cosmos
- Zinnia
- Sweet pea*
- Snapdragon*
- Ammi

- Monarda 'Bergamo'*
- *Rudbeckia hirta*
- Dianthus*
- Sunflower
- *Scabiosa atropurpurea* and *S. stellata*

* Best started under cover.

TOP LEFT Our Flower Farm zinnias are succession sown three or four times for months of colour.

TOP RIGHT Italian ranunculus will continue to flower with regular harvesting.

Watering

Seedlings are best watered from underneath by sitting the container in a pot or tray of water and allowing that water to soak up through the potting mix. Overhead watering spreads a disease called damping-off. The infected seedlings germinate but the stem tissue at the soil line rots and the seedlings collapse, beyond salvage. Start again after ensuring trays and equipment are well washed and disinfected to avoid infecting future crops.

Hardening off

Before planting in the garden, gradually acclimatise the seedlings to outdoor conditions in a process called 'hardening off'. For about a week, sit the seedlings in a sheltered place for a few hours a day. Slowly increase the amount of time they are outside. Once they are tough enough to be permanently outside, into the garden bed they go.

Propagation techniques

Once you've had success growing easy varieties, try cut flowers that are a little more demanding such as echinops, aquilegia and echinacea. For successful germination of tricker varieties, you'll need to know:

- The right depth to sow the seeds

- Whether germination requires light or dark

- The ideal temperature for germination

- Whether cold stratification is needed. Seeds from cold climates may need this.

- Whether smoke treatment is required. Australian or South African natives may need this (see p. 194).

RIGHT Aquilegia is a surprisingly good cut flower. It is available as plants from garden centres or you can grow your own from seed.

Seed Starting Supplies
Basics

Stock up on these basic supplies for growing from seed:

- Seed-raising mix. Shop-bought seed-starter mix has been sterilised so should be free of weed seeds, insects, mould and pathogens. If using homemade compost, sieve to remove lumps, then mix in some sharp sand to help with drainage. Soil should be light and friable (free draining) to enable healthy root development.

- Vermiculite. To cover and protect the sown seeds and help retain moisture.

- Seed trays, plug trays (also called flats), terracotta pots or recycled containers with drainage holes.

- A container to hold the seed tray or pot, so seedlings can be watered from below.

- Liquid seaweed fertiliser. Shop-bought seed-starter mix has low fertility, and seedlings will require supplementary nutrition. Use a simple pump spray dispenser and apply a weak seaweed solution to the seedlings once a week.

- Labels and a permanent UV stable pen.

Advanced supplies

- A propagation station. Comprises a simple heat mat and dome to retain humidity and ensure the potting mix doesn't dry out. Controlling the temperature of the soil with a heat mat allows for faster germination and a higher success rate. Remove the dome once the seedlings have germinated to increase airflow and avoid the risk of damping-off.

- Lighting. If you've outgrown a crowded sunny windowsill but don't have a greenhouse, hang simple fluorescent shop lights in a shed, garage or basement and place the seed trays underneath. For best results drop the lights to 15 centimetres above the seedlings. The light produces heat, drying out the potting mix, so check moisture levels regularly.

- Seed sowing chutes. Either manual or battery-operated for sowing fine seed. If you don't have a chute, carefully place the seeds in the fold of a piece of paper and push the seeds out one by one with the end of a pencil.

Soil Blocking

The secret to successful seed sowing

Soil blocks are small individual cubes of compressed potting mix made with a special tool, called a soil blocker. Seeds are sown into the top of each soil block and the ice-cube shaped blocks stand up neatly with no need for a container or pot.

It takes a little practice to get the proportions of potting mix to water exactly right so that the cubes hold their shape. The soil blocks are pushed out of the tool into a tray and are watered from below. As the seeds germinate and seedlings grow, the roots are naturally air pruned where they protrude from the soil block. This helps encourage root branching leading to better root growth. Once the seedling is large enough, it can be planted out into the garden bed, soil block and all, without disturbing the roots. Growers have found that seedlings grow faster this way and result in bigger, healthier plants.

Here's how to soil block:

- Moisten the potting mix (no need to use special seed-raising mix) with warm water so a squeezed handful of mix almost drips (but not quite).

- Press the soil blocker firmly into the mix, pushing down several times so the tool fills with potting mix.

- Remove any excess mix from the bottom of the soil blocker with a flat blade; a butter knife is perfect.

- Press out your soil blocks into a flat container capable of holding water.

- Rinse your soil blocking tool after each use.

- Sow 1–2 seeds per soil block and cover in line with the seed packet instructions.

- Water from below, gently draining any excess water.

A Manageable Cutting Garden

Cut flowers can be grown almost anywhere. In pots by the front door, among existing plants and shrubs in a garden border or in a dedicated area, such as a raised bed in the vegetable garden.

If growing within established garden beds, plant annual flowers in colour combinations that complement your existing shrubs and perennials. Growing cut flowers in a dedicated space can allow you to experiment with bolder colour combinations while minimising the visual impact of stakes, irrigation and labels. But there's no reason cutting gardens can't be both beautiful and productive. Use foraged branches as stakes to support climbing sweet peas or tie up plants with biodegradable jute string.

The less space you have, the more selective and diligent you need to be. Growing in pots requires successions of seedlings or small plants on standby to refresh the display as older flowers fade. In small spaces, gaps and dying plants are far more noticeable. Like any professional flower farmer, you need to be a little ruthless. Plants past their peak production should be removed and composted so the bed or pot can be readied for the next variety.

If you have oodles of space, it's important to be realistic about how much time and energy you have. A raised bed the size of a large dining table, in full sun, will generally be sufficient to grow flowers for your home for a large part of the year. Double that space if you want multiple colour combinations. Planting will be tight, closer than recommended by the seed suppliers, but with good soil preparation and clever planning this small space will produce buckets of flowers over an extended period.

Making it manageable:

- Start small and scale up.

- Grow a mix of annuals, biennials and labour-saving perennials.

- Forage from existing trees and shrubs.

- Prioritise CCA flowers.

- Evaluate flowers each season to assess their usefulness against the time and resources they take to grow.

Cut flower self-seeders

Self-sown plants (or 'volunteers' as they are known in the US) are often tougher and hardier than their parent plants. However, cultivars with specifically bred petal shapes or colourings dwindle in prevalence over time as plants revert to type. Plant new seed if you must have a specific shade or petal shape. Sweet peas are the exception to this rule as they almost always stay true to type. To encourage self-seeding:

- Weed carefully. Newly emerged self-seeders often resemble weeds. Learn to identify the leaves of young volunteer plants. Take a photo on your phone for future reference.

- At the end of the growing season leave seed heads on plants, a source of future volunteers and food for the birds.

- Collect ripe seed to scatter in garden beds. The success rate is generally much lower than sowing seed under cover but it's worth a try.

- Don't till the soil. A shallow layer of compost laid on top of the garden bed will prevent seeds from becoming buried too deeply. Some seeds need light to germinate, so skip the compost in this instance.

- Choose polite self-seeders rather than garden thugs.

High and low maintenance plants

At the Flower Farm, plants fall into four categories:

High maintenance

- **Hero plants.** Dahlias are the most labour-intensive, requiring a year-round rota of tasks. However, they are the Flower Farm's favourite, and our customers love growing their own. The annual tuber sale is highly anticipated with the most coveted varieties selling out in minutes. Year-round commitment is also required for heirloom chrysanthemums with seasonal tasks including rooting cuttings, planting out, staking, pinching, disbudding and corralling.

Moderate maintenance

- **Annuals.** Crops grown from seed such as snapdragons and sweet peas need careful tending as seedlings but are easy-going once established. They are cheap and quick to grow.

Low maintenance

- **Perennials.** Plants such as roses, geraniums, salvias and echinacea are more expensive than seed but require little more than a yearly feed, prune and weed once established.

Ultra-low maintenance

- **Self-sown.** Normally annuals and biennials, but sometimes also perennials, these plants have grown from seed dropped in the previous growing season. On the Flower Farm self-sown seedlings are thinned, leaving only the strongest. They lend bouquets a sense of cottage garden abundance, with a mix of umbel-shaped ammi flowers, sculptural poppy pods, spikes of larkspur, cheery calendula, and dainty feverfew.

Much of the romance of the typical cottage garden rests on self-seeders like these growing in natural drifts, popping up through cracks in the paving or nooks in stone walls.

- Scabiosa
- Poppies
- Calendula
- Sweet peas (annual and perennial)
- Feverfew
- Verbascum
- Queen Anne's lace (ammi)
- Sweet rocket

ABOVE *Verbascum hybridum* 'Southern Charm' is a much-appreciated self-seeder.

Check first – weed or volunteer?

Across the world gardeners are faced with the dilemma of introduced garden plants escaping into forest, bush and wetlands, outcompeting endemic species and depriving birds, insects and wild animals of habitat and food sources. Many of the most vigorous plants are highly ornamental and make great cut flowers, so it's very important to check a plant's status before establishing it in your garden. If it's a problem plant or designated weed in your region, find an alternative.

No Dig

The Flower Farm's war on weeding

The Flower Farm follows the principles of organic gardening with help from companion planting, natural fertilisers and good bugs.

To achieve a thriving garden buzzing with insects and birds, we were prepared to hand weed and tolerate the occasional nibbled flower. We reluctantly laid down weed mat (horticultural mat) but still the forest of weeds and grasses was undiminished, and weeding consumed our time. We had hoped to get on top of the seed bank in our first year. We were wrong.

Each time a crop finished we tilled in a generous layer of compost. While this added vital organic matter to the soil, improved fertility and the soil's ability to hold water, it also brought to the surface a whole new generation of weed and grass seeds. In due course these germinated and filled our days with ever more backbreaking hand weeding. We needed a circuit breaker.

The No Dig approach was trialled. In this method the soil is not disturbed (no digging, tilling or turning over). Instead, compost is laid on top and plants planted directly into that compost. The roots find their way into the soil beneath. This enriches the soil, reduces labour and smothers the weeds. Deprived of light, they are unable to germinate. If a bed is very weedy and you have good rainfall, cardboard can be lain over the soil before the compost is added.

No Dig Quick Steps

These initial steps delivered instant results on the Flower Farm:

- Areas around perennial shrubs including roses and native trees are covered with a thin layer of cardboard to block out the light, preventing the germination and growth of weeds.

- When a crop is finished, the weed mat is pulled back and the fading plants are mown or cut back with a whipper-snipper (strimmer) rather than being pulled from the ground. This serves two purposes – roots rot, enriching the soil, and cut stems act as a mulch.

- Over this layer of natural mulch, we apply a layer of compost, then drench the soil with a liquid seaweed solution or compost tea. This hastens the decomposition of the mulch.

- The weed mat is laid back on top of the bed and new seedlings popped in next to the decaying roots and cut stalks of last season's crop.

The same process works equally well without a weed mat.

Cutting Garden Toolkit

Good-quality, strong tools are essential in a manageable cutting
garden. Tasks will take you less time and be easier on your body.
This is particularly the case for repetitive tasks like planting bulbs
or pruning dormant roses. The following are particularly useful:

Multipurpose

Hori-hori knife	This Japanese knife has a concave steel blade with one straight edge and the other serrated. Use it for digging, cutting, dividing perennials, weeding, transplanting and even bulb planting due to its handy depth gauge.
Strong secateurs	Good-quality secateurs with sharp blades make light work of rose pruning, cutting woody stems and harvesting foliage.
Foldable saw	Useful for cutting anything too wide or tough for the secateurs, including big dahlia clumps and larger branches.

Planting

Dibber	Use to make holes in the soil for small bulbs, seedlings and rooted cuttings.
Hamilton tree planter	This simple and effective tool was initially acquired for planting trees but is also great for planting big bulbs including amaryllis, hyacinths and daffodils. The higher-tech Pottiputki is also recommended and widely available.
Apple corer	An effective alternative to the dibber, inspired by the Hamilton tree planter, a corer removes a piece of soil perfectly sized for popping in a seedling plug. Works best with damp soil (all seedlings should be planted into damp soil).
Butter knife	The perfect tool for easing seedlings out of little pots before planting out. If you can't find one at the back of your cutlery drawer, check out antique or bric-a-brac shops.
Bulb trowel	Perfect for small quantities of larger bulbs. We make a slit in the ground, push the soil back with the blade of the trowel and pop the bulb in, with minimal soil disturbance.

Weeding

Mini scythe	Use to quickly remove annual weeds when they're tiny. We gently run this handheld tool over the surface of the soil thereby disturbing it as little as possible while ensuring that the weed seedlings are detached from their roots and die. Perennial weeds or those with a tap root are harder to eliminate and will need to be dug from the ground.
Pronged weeder	Weeding tool of choice for tough perennial weeds. Enables weeding around a flowering plant without disturbing that plant's roots.
Spade	For digging dahlias and other clumping plants.

Hamilton tree planter

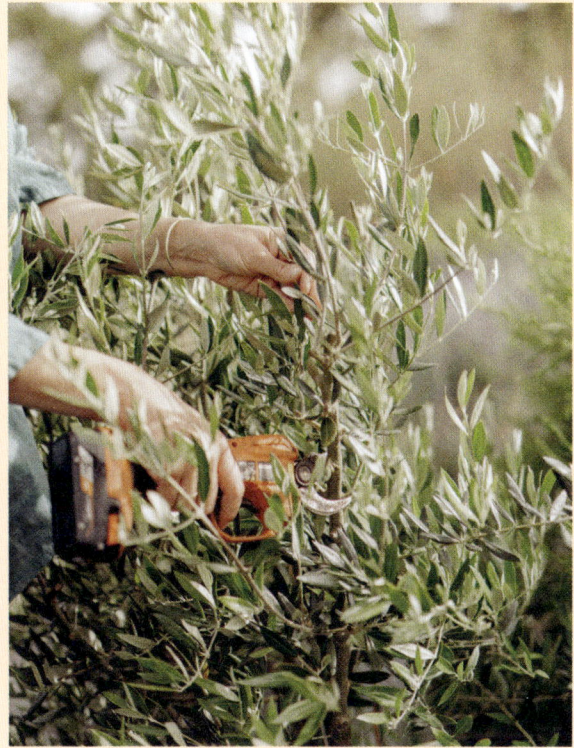

Mechanical secateurs

Cutting / Harvesting

Needle-nosed snips	Lightweight and spring-loaded, with precise pointy tips that make harvesting easier and allow for far greater accuracy.
De-thorner	For de-thorning roses at picking time, as roses with thorns have a shorter vase life and are harder to handle. Can also be used to remove the lower leaves of cut stems.
Bucket trolley	Saves your back when carrying heavy buckets of water. And it's easier to place the cut stems directly into water when the buckets are higher off the ground.

Mechanical

Mechanical secateurs	Like those used by vineyard workers, light enough to use all day. For pruning fruit trees and harvesting tough Australian and South African native shrubs.
Hedge trimmer	For harvesting lavender, statice and billy buttons and cutting back achillea and other perennials in early winter. Useful when harvesting large quantities of flowers for drying.
Trolley sprayer	No chemicals are used on the Flower Farm but we love this tool to spray the good stuff like seaweed foliar feed and well-strained compost and nettle teas.

A Perfect Cut Flower

Commercial growing has changed the way most of us buy flowers. Almost any type of cut stem seems to be available at almost any time of the year. Roses in the middle of winter, tulips in autumn. Seasonality has become disconnected from flower growing.

For commercial hothouse growers, a critical factor is not a flower's scent or delicate beauty, but the cut stem's ability to be out of water for long periods, and a robust tolerance for rattling around in a plane's cargo hold. Flowers can be up to a week old when they arrive in our home from the supermarket or florist, so vase life (the length of time a flower will survive once it has been harvested) has understandably become an obsession for breeders.

Vase life

The home gardener can afford to be much less fussy about vase life, popping outside to cut seasonal flowers at any time. Vase life remains a consideration, though, especially if you intend to give bunches to friends or even sell your stems at markets. However, growing your own allows time and space for those delightfully ephemeral flowers rarely seen in stores. We adore these fleeting beauties:

- Iceland poppies
- Sweet peas
- Open-centred, fragrant roses
- Single dahlias
- Blossom branches
- Flowering magnolia
- Clematis
- Verbascum
- Verbena

LEFT The sky-blue spike of *Salvia uliginosa* didn't make the grade for bouquets but is great for events.

TOP RIGHT Double cosmos in a rustic jug.

Double trouble

Double flowers often last longer in a vase than their single-flowered equivalents, for varying reasons:

- Some double varieties are sterile.
- Plant breeding has created double varieties where the mutated plant parts become petaloids (rather than true petals) often lasting longer on the stem.
- In others, the double petals hinder a pollinator's access to the flower thereby delaying or preventing pollination.
- Double flowers tend to be more robust and can withstand adverse weather.

If you're picking for extra vase life, make it a double.

Flowering window

Some flowers can remain on the plant for weeks before being harvested and still have a long vase life. Sweet William, billy buttons and paper daisies are great examples. Others, such as tulips, have a very narrow flowering window – sometimes as little as a day – before the flowers are too open to be picked and vase life is compromised. A shorter flowering window makes harvesting a challenge, so if you are growing flowers for a specific event a long flowering window will make it easier to match flowering time and event date.

Sometimes a long flowering window compensates for a short vase life. Dainty Iceland poppies in bewitching sherbet tones have a short vase life. Yet they have a wonderfully long flowering window – up to 3 months on the farm with regular deadheading. Incredibly useful for weddings and events and a favourite to press as a dried flower or pop in a little vase on the desk.

	Vase life	Flowering window*
Tulip	7 days	1–7 days
Stocks	7–9 days	2–3 weeks
Iceland poppy	2–4 days	2–3 months
Italian ranunculus	7 days	1–3 months
Dahlia	5 days	3–5 months
Lilium	10–12 days	2–3 weeks
Alstroemeria	10 days	2–4 months

(*weather dependent)

Stem length

Most flowers grown for cutting should have stems at least 45 centimetres long, the minimum requirement for a hand-tied bouquet. And because stems are rarely cut at ground level, this means the plants need to be even taller, at least 50 centimetres. Remember to take prevailing conditions into account, as this affects how large the plants will grow. Soils with lower fertility or reduced water will produce smaller, shorter plants.

Before buying, check the dimensions of the plant on the seed packet or plant label as height and size can vary dramatically between cultivars. Longer stems are easier to use in arrangements, but don't exclude plants on stem length alone. Many spring bulbs have short stems and happily fill bud vases or make dainty posies. Float flower heads in bowls of water or even thread petite flowers into large arrangements by using water tubes on spikes (also known as water picks).

Tip: *If you are growing in pots, don't focus so much on stem length – big plants can become unwieldy. Instead, plant dwarf varieties and fill your containers with a mix of diminutive treasures such as pansies, lovely trailing phlox and dwarf single dahlias.*

ABOVE Two zinnia flowers side by side. One is 80 centimetres tall, the other just 25 centimetres. One will provide buckets of flowers for use in dozens of bunches, the other will be limited to bud vases.

The perfect cut flower

The perfect cut flower is ready for cutting when it's needed (timing made easier by a long flowering window); and provides the desirable stem length, vase life, scent, colour and overall aesthetic. Consider how you'll be using your cut flowers:

	Focus	Less important	Aim for
For the home or close friends	Grow what you love. Prioritise fragrance (but consider allergy sufferers). Aim to regularly refresh your vases with seasonal flowers and when there isn't much in the garden beds, cut a bunch of foliage.	Stem length isn't important if you're filling bud vases or making long and low centrepieces for the dining table but is necessary for large vases. Vase life matters less if you're happy to refresh regularly but aim for at least 5 days.	Aim for something new to cut every month. Make a flower planner.
For gift bunches or to sell to a florist	Vase life of at least a week. Stem length over 45 cm. Bright colours or on-trend combinations. CCAs.	Vines, climbers, creepers or anything with a very fine or delicate stem could be hard to use.	Aim for flowers you can't buy from your local florist or supermarket.
For drying	Flowers that hold their colour and form when dried and which store well for future use.	Stem length isn't important as you can wire dried flowers for a longer stem.	Aim for boxes full to bursting with dried stems by late autumn.
For adding colour and interest to your garden	Flowers that you can enjoy both in the landscape and as a cut flower. Perennial shrubs that respond well to pruning.	One-cut varieties like tulips are less important in this context. You want repeat flowerers so you can have colour in the garden and the vase.	Aim for enough flowers that cutting stems for a big vase won't make a dent in the garden bed.
For a wedding or event	Grow premium, hard-to-find, delicate flowers in carefully curated colours. Ensure they will be flowering at the right time of year.	A 2-day vase life is generally sufficient. Avoid flowers that are not considered premium (such as regular zinnias or sunflowers).	Aim for a realistic target. Rather than growing every flower, prioritise. Be led by the colour scheme.

Optimum harvesting time

The best time to cut is early in the morning before the sun is up. The flowers are most likely to be fully hydrated at this time. Outside winter, try not to pick in the middle of the day. The warmer the day, the earlier you pick. If you do have to cut in the heat, get the flowers out of the sun as soon as possible and let them rest for several hours in cool water in a dark place before arranging. When cutting lots of flowers, start with those that are most heat sensitive and move them out of the sun to somewhere cool for a big drink.

If a heatwave is predicted, it's worth cutting anything with a long vase life (such as lisianthus) a few days in advance. Also harvest flowers with white or light petals as these can turn brown in hot summer winds. For repeat flowering plants such as dahlias, deadhead after the heat has passed.

Impending rain is another consideration. While morning dew is fine, water-drenched flower heads are more likely to rot or snap. Harvest before the rain arrives. If you don't beat the storm, wait until the flowers have dried before cutting.

In cool climates, the first major autumn frost is sometimes called a killing frost. While this can catch gardeners by surprise, if you do have advance warning, rush out and grab the last bunch of the season. And remember to set an early alarm the next day, morning sun sparkling on frost-covered flowers is such a lovely sight.

RIGHT Lisianthus, dahlias and Queen Anne's lace in the flower studio having a big drink before being arranged.

OPPOSITE Little milk bottles with single stems of flowers make a great table runner. Pictured are cosmos, feverfew, geranium, echinacea, honesty and foxglove.

Just add water

Trugs of cut flowers are the stuff of cottage garden romance, and look wonderful in a photo, but it's not the best way to achieve optimum vase life.

How you cut and condition your flowers is exceptionally important. Whether you're harvesting a flower grown for cutting or snipping foliage from an existing shrub in your garden, the way you handle that cut stem has a huge impact on how good it will look in the vase.

When cutting flowers, have a bucket of water by your side. If you're harvesting short stems, carry a jug or jam jar instead. Immediately after the stem is cut, strip off the lower leaves, immature flower buds and unwanted extra side branches before plunging the stem into a bucket of cool, clean water.

Clean vases

After your flowers have rested in a bucket in a cool place for an hour or more, recut the stem ends on a 45-degree angle and arrange into vases that are squeaky clean. If the glass is cloudy or feels slimy when wet, give it another scrub. This residue is evidence of bacteria that will result in foul water and dead flowers. When drawn up the stem, bacteria block the xylem, preventing water from reaching the flower.

We clean our vases and buckets with soapy water (dish soap is fine). It can be a challenge to clean vases with narrow necks. For these and other tricky vessels, use bottle brushes or sanitising tablets made for cleaning baby bottles and follow the packet instructions.

Remember, naturally grown flowers are thirsty, and drink much more than hothouse flowers purchased from the supermarket. Keep vases topped up and change the water every couple of days.

Flower food – should you use it?

We all want our cut flowers to last as long as possible and it's good to have a solution to a problem, especially if it's as simple as snipping the corner off a sachet and tipping the contents into a vase. Quick, easy, job done – or is it? Proprietary flower foods vary but generally contain the following:

- Sugar to feed the flower.
- Crystaline bleach to act as a biocide, killing bacteria from the decaying plant material and sugar.
- Citric acid to acidify the pH in the vase, making a less attractive environment for bacterial growth.

Bleach works but we are not fans. It has a detrimental effect on septic systems or eventually finds its way into our waterways. Instead, we add a good splash of vinegar to vase water. Roughly 5 tablespoons of vinegar to 2 litres of water.

Other than sweet peas, which last an extra day or two with a teaspoon of sugar syrup added to vase water, vase life tests have shown sugar to be broadly unnecessary. And as sugar increases the rate of bacterial growth in water, it may even compromise vase life.

Be sure to rest flowers in a cool place before arranging – leave overnight in a laundry rather than a room with a fire and avoid windowsills in full sun.

Plant biology – the science behind long-lasting flowers

Plant stems contain several tube-like drinking straws called xylem. As the plant transpires, losing water from the stomata in the leaves, negative pressure draws water up the xylem tubes in the stem from the root system. Water ensures the cells in the leaves, stem and flowers remain turgid and prevents any part of the plant from wilting.

As soon as the stem is cut, the connection to the root system and water source is removed. The leaves will continue to transpire and if there is no water, air will be sucked up into the xylem tubes instead. Just like an airlock in your home plumbing system, this air bubble will prevent water from reaching the flower head, causing it to flop and significantly reducing vase life.

A Beautiful and Balanced Bouquet

Choosing 'ingredients' from your cutting garden to make a beautiful bouquet can be confusing, even intimidating. Often, we cut what catches our attention without thinking about how the various elements will work together. This easy mantra will help: **'Focal, Filler, Foliage'**.

Focal flowers

Focal flowers take centre stage in any arrangement, their size drawing the eye. Favourites include dahlias, roses, heirloom chrysanthemums, hydrangeas and Italian ranunculus. We also love sunflowers, globe alliums, proteas and banksias. And because focal flowers are the star turn, many are perfectly wonderful by themselves in a vase without filler or foliage:

- Long-stemmed Oriental lilies in a tall glass vase with crystal-clear water.

- A ceramic jug of tulips, straight stemmed at first but ready to bend and walk around the vase as soon as your back is turned.

- A mass of mixed garden roses in different pastel colours, placed discreetly on a side table, filling the room with fragrance.

RIGHT Long-stemmed garden roses have a timeless elegance. Remove the thorns for easier arranging and longer vase life.

OPPOSITE Popular blue gum is as much loved for its fragrance as for the milky-blue leaves.

Filler flowers

These smaller flowers fill the spaces between the large focal flowers in a mixed bunch, providing a finer texture and adding a second or third colour to the arrangement. Select wisely and you'll be able to alter the mood and style of the arrangement, even when using the same focal flower (see p. 53).

Foliage

Foliage is much more than an afterthought. Adding structure, interest and sometimes fragrance, it's the backbone of an arrangement. Complement focal and filler flowers by selecting foliage that naturally grows with those flowers and create a garden in a vase.

- Scented pelargonium with roses for a cottage garden bouquet.

- Glossy magnolia leaves with white hydrangea for a clean, modern look.

- Lush, dark-leaved cinnamon basil to add drama to a romantic rose bouquet.

An unexpected or arresting choice of foliage can dramatically lift a bouquet. Try pairing tulips with banksia foliage. The contrast between the clean, squeaky leaves of the tulips and the coarse textured, zigzag banksia leaves couldn't be greater. Yet it's an inspired pairing with plenty of wow factor.

By varying the foliage, you can make the same focal and filler flowers sing very different tunes. Excellent when you are awash with dahlias or roses but want to create a selection of moods in your arrangements. And it's equally useful when flowers are thin on the ground. A vase of only foliage, perhaps eucalyptus or olive, can be very sophisticated and given the monochromatic palette, very soothing.

Foliage has a very practical role in an arrangement. The woodier stems provide support for large, heavy flower heads and add structure to a bouquet. Placed between the focal flowers, foliage helps separate the blooms, creating space.

A few extra stems of foliage can quickly increase the size of a bouquet. Foliage-heavy arrangements are very popular in line with the trend towards natural, organic, loose bunches. If in doubt we always add more foliage.

Often overlooked is the important role foliage can play in providing fragrance. Unscented flowers, including dahlias, benefit from being paired with scented foliage such as rose geranium, lemon verbena or flowering basil. Scented flowers work well with herbal foliage – think parsley, coriander, lemon balm or rosemary. On the Flower Farm native Australian trees and shrubs add a unique set of fragrances, from the menthol scent of eucalyptus and tea tree to the more floral notes of myrtle, Geraldton wax and thryptomene.

Focal, Filler, Foliage for every season*

	Focal	Filler	Foliage
Spring	Italian ranunculus Tulip	Larkspur Linaria	Bells of Ireland Parsley
Summer	Rose Lily	Gypsophila (baby's breath) Paper daisy	Blue gum Olive
Autumn	Dahlia Heirloom chrysanthemum	Marigold Rudbeckia Zinnia	Scented geranium Pittosporum
Winter	Protea Ornamental kale	Wallflower Stock	Bracken fern Banksia foliage

*Seasonal variation according to climate.

Flower shape

The current fashion is for round-shaped flowers. Italian ranunculus, round dahlias and ball-shaped chrysanthemums are particularly popular.

While large focal flowers in other shapes, including lilies, cactus dahlias and spider chrysanthemums, are less popular, they can add variety and visual interest to a mixed arrangement.

Shape	Purpose	Examples
Round	Perfect in a typical rounded bunch. Often focal flowers.	Roses, round dahlias, ranunculus
Globe	Eye catching and a bit of fun.	Allium, echinops, ball and pompon dahlias and chrysanthemums
Daisy	Large flowers are great on their own. Smaller flowers make effective fillers.	Echinacea, rudbeckia, sunflowers, anemones, feverfew
Line / Spike	Adds height and excitement and creates vertical accents.	Delphinium, larkspur, liatris, veronica, snapdragon, foxglove
Plume	Adds fine texture and movement.	Celosia, astilbe, grasses
Umbel / Flat Head	Great for filling gaps between focal flowers. The horizontal plane gives the eye a resting point.	Yarrow, ammi, *Daucus carota*, sedum, fennel, parsley, Queen Anne's lace
Bells	Used in a similar way to a line flower but softer while still adding height.	Canterbury bells, bells of Ireland, lily of the valley
Trumpets	A different shape of focal flower. Attention seekers.	Lilies, gladioli, alstromeria

CLOCKWISE FROM TOP LEFT
Flower shapes: umbel, daisy, spike and bells

Airy elements

Airy elements are easy to forget but so important, adding movement to an arrangement and evoking the sense of the garden in which they grew. These flowers can be transformative:

- Larkspur 'White Cloud'
- Geraldton wax (*Chamelaucium uncinatum*)
- Baby's breath (*Gypsophila*)
- Columbine or Granny's bonnets (*Aquilegia*)
- Burnet (*Sanguisorba*)

Vines

Trailing plants are not widely available from flower wholesalers; growing your own is yet another way to add a point of difference. Tumbling over the edge of a container, trailing plants and vines break the line between flowers and vase, thereby connecting the two. And the wild, straight-from-the-garden look makes them valuable in natural designs. We love:

Foliage	Flowers
Hyacinth bean	Sweet pea (annual and perennial)
Love in a puff	Jasmine
Ivy	Clematis
Cherry tomatoes on the vine	Nasturtium
Raspberry	Climbing roses
Grapevine	Bougainvillea
Glory vine	Honeysuckle
Creeping fig	Trailing phlox

Texture

As the flower farming movement grows around the world, texture has emerged as an important consideration in the plant mix. The coolest florists are incorporating soft and coarse foliage, rough-edged leaves, dried grasses, juicy succulents and woody cones and nuts. Texture provides a fun element and is the perfect excuse to head out foraging.

Texture	Effect	Foliage	Flowers
Fine	Calming, softening, delicate	Dusty miller, fern, ivy	Queen Anne's lace, small flowers like astilbe or yarrow
Coarse	Dramatic, exciting, organic and contrasting	Branches including curly willow, bark, pine or banksia cones, seed pods, magnolia, gourds	Banksia, protea, thistles like sea holly or echinops, artichokes

'Francis Meilland' roses pair with different filler flowers to achieve very different effects.

TOP LEFT Hot pink cosmos and zinnias create a fun, bubble-gum look, perfect for birthday bunches.

TOP RIGHT Dried grass heads with dark stems give an architectural, minimalist effect.

BOTTOM RIGHT Cottage garden perennials such as astilbe and sedum add gentle raspberry tones to this soft arrangement.

BOTTOM LEFT Dusty pink lisianthus with burgundy centres add a more refined, elegant, bridal feel.

TOP LEFT Rich, jewel tones and lots of texture from dahlias, amaranthus, echinops, verbena and lisianthus.

BOTTOM LEFT Wiring flowers to support stems and avoid breakages.

TOP RIGHT Bouquet adjustments.

BOTTOM RIGHT Buttonholes to suit the colour scheme.

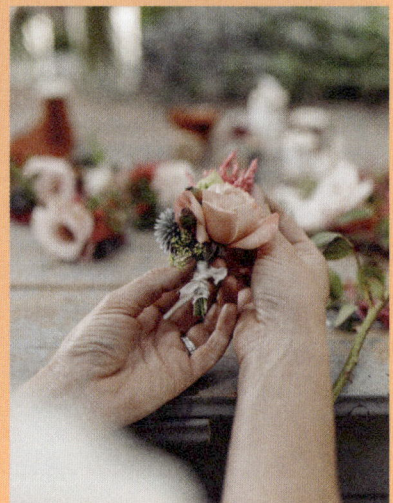

Growing Your Own Wedding Bouquet

Many people fall in love with flowers after choosing what to hold or wear on this very special day. If you decide to make your own bouquet (or one for a family member or friend), be sure to give yourself plenty of time. Ideally, you'll have access to a large garden (more choice) and a loose design brief in case the season is late/early or other adverse weather events occur.

Have a back-up plan in the form of a secondary flower supplier. If nothing else, this will ease the pressure and make the whole experience more enjoyable. Even if the bouquet features only a few stems you have grown yourself it will be so much more special as a result. Choose a range of plants that:

- Are in season where you live at the time you are getting married

- Grow well in your climate

- Have a long flowering window (e.g. dahlias)

- Are cut and come again (e.g. zinnias, Italian ranunculus or cosmos)

- You have some experience of growing or have already established in your garden (e.g. roses)

- Do well out of water (e.g. lisianthus, sea holly).

Plan when to plant by researching the number of 'days to maturity' from sowing to flowering and sow several successions of seeds to create a wider flowering window.

Practise making bouquets, buttonholes and table arrangements, honing your technique, in the weeks and months before the wedding. Even using different seasonal flowers, you'll become more adept at learning how many focal, filler and foliage stems you will need per arrangement. If you don't have flowers to hand, use foliage from trees and shrubs. The more you practise, the easier the big day will be.

Have you ever seen a florist put together a bunch of flowers? They make it look incredibly easy because they know where to place flowers, have developed strong hands that can hold multiple stems at once and store 'recipes' in their head, helping them to know what flowers work well together. So much of flower arranging is down to practice, experimenting and developing a personal aesthetic.

Seasonal Tasks

If you can't wait to begin growing flowers, these seasonal tasks and planting suggestions can help jumpstart your cutting garden. They are based on an 'average' year for climatic conditions on the Flower Farm but are applicable in many areas. If it is particularly hot or cold, wet or dry where you live, consult growing advice specific to your area.

Spring

Order now	Groundwork
• Summer flowering bulbs such as lilies and gladioli. Amaryllis bulbs for Christmas displays (southern hemisphere). • The last of the dahlia tubers. • Young plants such as clematis, penstemon and rudbeckia. • Flower seedlings for immediate planting.	• Weed or cover exposed areas especially before thistles and the like grow too large. • Mulch once the soil warms but while it's still moist. • Get irrigation organised (do this in winter for warm climates). • If gardening in a cold climate, prune the roses. If gardening in a warm climate, fertilise them.
Sow now	**Plant now**
• Raise seedlings of annuals such as cosmos, ageratum, statice, paper daisy and rudbeckia. • Direct sow sunflowers and zinnias once all risk of frost has passed.	• Drought-hardy plants like lavender, salvias and scented geranium, but remember to water well until they're established. • Dahlia tubers once the ground is damp rather than wet. • Summer bulbs as soon as they arrive.

Summer

Order now	Groundwork
• Spring bulbs such as Italian ranunculus, tulips, anemones and Dutch iris. • Shrubs and perennial plants for autumn planting like bare-root roses, Australian and South African natives, hydrangeas, viburnum. • Autumn flowering bulbs such as lycoris and nerine. Plant as soon as they arrive for flowers the same year.	• Keep up the watering and water ahead of heatwaves and hot spells rather than during. • Feed your plants with a liquid seaweed fertiliser. • Stake plants such as dahlias as they grow.
Sow now	**Forage**
• While it's not the best time for seed sowing, heat-tolerant plants with big seeds such as zinnias and sunflowers can survive if you water daily while they're small (second sowing if you planted in spring). • Herbs like basil and coriander, which are edible until they bolt, then use flower heads in arrangements. • Raise biennials from seed, ready to plant out during early autumn.	• Look for grasses that have gone to seed. Harvest and hang to dry for dried flower arrangements. • Harvest foliage, lavender and salvia for drying.

Autumn

Order now	Groundwork
• Seeds for autumn and spring sowing. • Bare-root roses.	• Dig and divide your dahlia tubers when the plants have died back. • Stay on top of weeds. • Add a layer of compost to newly cleared beds. • Sow a cover crop.
Sow now	**Plant now**
• Cold-hardy annuals and winter flowering plants like ornamental kale, snapdragons, calendula and scented stocks. • Winter colour for the tops of bulb pots including pansies, violas and nasturtiums. • Perennials you want to grow from seed, so they have a chance to establish before the cooler winter weather. Billy buttons, kangaroo paw, rudbeckia or echinacea.	• Spring bulbs including anemones, Italian ranunculus, cottage gladioli or Dutch iris. • Make a bulb lasagne (see p. 64) if space is tight. • Perennials sourced from a good nursery to plant out as the weather cools. Pay attention to filler and foliage plants.

Winter

Order now	Groundwork
• Dahlia tubers. • Rooted chrysanthemum cuttings. • Seeds for summer and autumn flowering annuals.	• Stay on top of weeds. • Add a layer of compost to all remaining beds. • Prune your roses (wait until spring in cold climates) and divide congested perennials and dahlia clumps. • If gardening in a warm climate, get irrigation organised and ready for heat in spring and summer.
Sow now	**Plant now**
• Raise seedlings of hardy annuals such as sweet pea, cornflower or scabiosa to plant out. • Direct sow cool-loving seeds like larkspur, delphinium and Iceland poppy.	• Bare-root roses (wait until spring in cold climates). • Peonies (if your winters are cold enough). • Australian and South African native plants.

FOLLOWING PAGE, CLOCKWISE FROM TOP LEFT
Sweetpeas; amaranthus; wattle; callistemon.

Four seasons of flowers

Spring.

The Secret to a Beautiful Spring

The secret to a beautiful spring cutting garden is planning ahead. During the warm days of late summer, surrounded by dahlias, zinnias and rudbeckias, it's hard to think beyond winter and as far forward as spring. But plan you must.

Spring flowering bulbs are ordered at the height of summer, a crazily busy period in the garden when there's precious little time to sit down and scan bulb catalogues and their dizzying array of flowers.

But it's so important to get ahead of these pre-ordering tasks if you want to secure the most sought-after colours and shapes, as these are quickly snapped up. Make a big note in your diary: Order bulbs! And sign up to the newsletters of the best growers in your area. Most companies email subscribers as soon as a new range is released. First in, best dressed.

In most places, spring flowering bulbs are planted in autumn. If you have exceptionally cold or wet winters, you might need to wait until early spring to plant the less hardy bulbs or those susceptible to rot.

And while these spring chapters cover everything you'll need for a bouquet or larger arrangement, sometimes the best spring display is a simple bowl of tulips or a slender vase with one perfect daffodil. In spring, we are far more relaxed about stem length. Little pansies pair beautifully in bud vases with grape hyacinths (*Muscari*). Perfect for admiring in detail on a side table. Or plant crocus bulbs in little terracotta pots and when they flower bring the plants indoors. Lined up along the centre of the kitchen table, these dainty flowers are enchanting. These Flower Farm favourites should feature high on your shopping list:

- Italian ranunculus
- Double daffodils
- Peony tulips
- Ornithogalum

- Cottage gladioli
- Dutch iris
- De Caen anemones

LEFT Early spring in the studio with branches of apple blossom and purple-fringed Italian ranunculus.

ABOVE Firey orange tulips with chocolate, red and salmon ranunculus in this spring arrangement.

Great spring colour combinations

If the range of bulbs available feels overwhelming, settle on a colour scheme.

- Soft mixed pastels for delicate, romantic bunches.
- Happy yellows pair beautifully with blues and whites.
- Moody shades balance out fiery oranges and reds.
- White. There is something exquisite about a vase of pure white tulips.

Cook up a Bulb Lasagne

Spring bulbs happily grow in pots, making them a lovely way to welcome spring in porch displays, small gardens and even the most compact of balconies.

For an extended display, the Dutch developed the bulb lasagne, a multi-layered affair featuring several different flowers. The biggest bulbs are planted deeper down in the pot, the smaller bulbs more shallowly. The shoots of the deepest bulbs will happily bend around the others to emerge unscathed.

Three layers is a good number for large, deep containers providing you choose bulbs with different planting depths. Add some 'pot toppers' such as violas or cyclamen or even salad greens to add winter interest while waiting for the bulbs to flower.

Begin by filling the bottom of your container with potting mix. The bottom layer, at some 15 centimetres deep, might include daffodils, tulips or big alliums. Cover these with 5 centimetres of potting mix, before adding an upper layer, perhaps crocus, ranunculus or anemones. Finish with topper plants.

Bottom layer: Daffodil 'Acropolis'

↓

Middle layer: Italian ranunculus 'Salmon'

↓

Top layer: Muscari 'Baby's Breath'

↓

Topper plants: Viola 'Rococo Frilled Mix'

Bulb, Corm, Rhizome or Tuber?

What is the difference between corms, rhizomes, tubers and bulbs?
Gardeners collectively call them bulbs, but for the horticulturalist
the different terms have distinct meanings. All are underground stems,
not roots. These underground stems store nutrients, essential for the
plant to complete its life cycle.

True bulbs
(Tulips, hyacinths, daffodils and lilies)

True bulbs consist of layers of modified leaves and
contain a miniature flower or sprout in the centre.
The roots at the bottom of the bulb anchor the plant
to the ground and absorb water and nutrients.

Tubers
(Dahlias)

Tubers are underground stems with fleshy, food-
storing parts, and eyes from which new stems grow.

Rhizomes
(Canna lilies, bearded iris, ginger)

Rhizomes are bulb-like power packs that grow along
the soil surface. Growth buds form on a rhizome for
next year's leaves and flowers. The original rhizome
will not reflower and in time will need to be dug out.

Corms
(Ranunculus, crocus, freesia, gladioli)

Corms vary in appearance but are usually short,
squat stems filled with food-storage tissue. As the
leaves and flowers grow and absorb nutrients,
the corm shrivels and disappears. One or more
additional corms are produced through the growing
season enabling the plant to regenerate.

Hero Flower   Italian Ranunculus

CCA • long flowering • easy to grow • long vase life

focal • round • spring • dried • trending

Plant summary

Buy me	Plant me	I flower	Cut me
As dormant corms in summer and autumn. These curious corms resemble tiny octopuses. A range of colours is available online from pastel pinks to chocolate, red, and white with purple frills.	In autumn (warm climate) or spring (cold climate). Plant 5 cm deep with the 'octopus-like tentacles' facing down. Make sure the ground is free draining to avoid corm rot.	From early to late spring. The first cut stems are short, but stems lengthen as the season progresses. Keep cutting for repeat flowers. Warming weather will slow and eventually prevent flowering. Water in dry weather for taller stems and a longer flowering window.	For beautiful spring bunches. Use in place of peonies if your winters are not cold enough to grow these beauties. Hang fully open ranunculus upside down to air dry for gorgeous out-of-season colour.

Secrets of a Spring Queen

1 **Order right.**

Order the right variety of ranunculus. Traditional garden ranunculus don't make the best cut flower – a lower petal count means a shorter vase life. Recent breeding has resulted in the Italian ranunculus variety. It has longer, stronger stems and larger flowers, sometimes as wide as a teacup, in superb colours including salmon, violet, 'pastello' (a mix of pastels), chocolate and various pinks. The more stems that are cut, the quicker they are replaced during an 8-week flowering period. As the weather warms and flowering slows, Italian ranunculus show an entirely new aesthetic – relaxed and open with flower centres revealed – rather like anemones or Iceland poppies.

2 **A shortcut for warm climates.**

Ranunculus are tender plants and don't like frost. In cold places where heavy frosts persist into spring, ranunculus corms are soaked and pre-sprouted, then planted under cover (see box). Once the risk of frost has passed, the sprouted corms go outside into the ground. Like sowing seeds indoors while the weather is still frosty, this buys a few weeks head start.

In warmer, drier climates no such fuss is required. Although ranunculus corms are tender, they do cope with passing cool temperatures and work well when planted directly, without soaking, into the ground in autumn. But it is important that the soil is relatively free draining throughout winter as corms are rot prone. If you live in a warm place but have heavy clay or wet winter soils, grow ranunculus in pots.

LEFT Chocolate, salmon and pastel pink Italian ranunculus.

3 **From one plant to many.**   While the ranunculus is perennial and will flower year after year when left in the ground, it's a good idea to pull them up when the foliage has died back. This way corms can be divided for more plants next season. Gently prise the corms apart (don't cut), and store in boxes somewhere warm, dry and out of reach of mice.

4 **The marshmallow test.**   For the longest vase life, up to 10 days, harvest flowers at the open bud stage. When gently squeezed the flower bud should be tender to touch, not hard, and feel as squishy as a marshmallow. If you plan to dry stems, wait until the flower opens before cutting.

Grow Me Instead

If you live in a cold climate with a short spring season, ranunculus may not be a good choice. Consider instead the ravishing peony. These plants are exceptionally cold tolerant, requiring frost to flower, and a large percentage of the globe's commercially grown flowers hail from Alaska. There is a catch for the budding cut flower grower. Peony plants take between 3 and 5 years to begin producing flowers and there's no cut-and-come-again advantage: just one crop of gorgeous giant frilly flowers – the world's most sought-after cut stems.

If your growing conditions don't provide for the free-draining winter soils ranunculus require, grow the corms in pots or opt for these spring-flowering alternatives:

- Hot sunny areas – triteleia, ixia, sparaxis, Dutch iris, hyacinth and allium.

- Heavy clay and wet soils – camassia and *Fritillaria meleagris*.

- Shorter stems for windy places – Snowdrops, muscari, dwarf iris, miniature daffodils, short-stemmed double tulips.

OPPOSITE A spring vase of warm- and cool-toned flowers. Using ranunculus in yellows, oranges and purples acts as a bridge, connecting all flowers in the arrangement.

How to pre-sprout ranunculus

1   Soak corms for 3 to 4 hours in room temperature water, changing the water every hour. Any longer and the corms may rot.

2   Fill a tray with moist potting mix and lay the corms on top. Cover with a thin layer of potting mix.

3   Check the corms every couple of days. As they develop fine rootlets and little shoots, plant in pots and keep in a bright, frost-free place. Remove any that have rotted.

4   Plant into the garden once the risk of frost has passed. This process also works well for anemone corms.

Focal Flowers   Tulips

easy to grow • low water • cold tolerant

focal • spring • bulb • cup shaped

Plant summary

Buy me	Plant me	I flower	Cut me
As dormant bulbs in summer and autumn. Easily found in garden centres or online.	In autumn, twice the height of the bulb (three times in warm climates because the soil will be cooler). If soil is not free draining, plant bulbs in pots.	From early to late spring. If dry weather occurs in the month before flowering, water regularly for longer stems.	When the colour of the petals is just visible. This provides the longest vase life. For double or fringed varieties, wait an extra day to allow the flowers to develop fully. Only half fill the vase with water; the fleshy stems will rot if fully submerged.

Secrets of a Spring Classic

1 **Bold bulbs.**

Differentiate your flowers from the supermarket offering. Choose flame-throated parrot tulips, double peony-shaped varieties, streaked bicolour forms or frilled edges. But get in early; the best colours and varieties sell quickly. A stem length of 45 centimetres or more is important for bunches; shorter varieties can be grown in little pots.

2 **Plant tight.**

Very little space is required to grow tulips. Bulbs can be planted tight, as close as eggs in a box. Just make sure they don't touch. They are brilliant in pots if your outdoor space is confined to a balcony or terrace. Don't forget to water bulbs grown in pots; they can be dry even if it has recently rained.

3 **Extend the season.**

The flowering window for tulips can be short and an early burst of heat may result in all your tulips flowering at once. Extend the season by growing different varieties. Look for early, mid and late flowering varieties:

- The earliest are *Tulipa kaufmanniana* with their short stems and coloured leaves. Then Single Early and Double Early types and some Species tulips.

- Mid-season flowers are provided by the Parrot, Darwin Hybrid, Fringed, Lily Flowered and Triumph types.

- Late flowering tulips are the Single Late and Double Late groups together with more Species tulips.

LEFT A tulip extravaganza: the many forms, colours and sizes of tulips.

Store bulbs in a fridge (away from food) and plant in batches over a series of weeks. A hot, dry spell may spoil your plans but generally this strategy works well. One of the last tulips to flower, the Double or Peony Tulip, is also one of the longest lasting. Breeding has created double petals at the centre of the flower. This mutation means no nectar for the bees, and because the flowers are not pollinated, they last much longer in the garden and vase.

4 Don't cut your tulips.

For the home gardener tulip bulbs can be expensive, and each produces only one flower. The commercially grown tulips sold in shops are managed in a very specific way. Treated as an annual flower, they are harvested with the bulb still attached. This allows for the longest possible stem length and means the flowers can be dry stored (bulb and all) in big refrigerators where they are wrapped tightly in paper, laid horizontally on racks and held like this for weeks. As they are needed, the flowers are brought out of the fridge, the bulb is cut off, and the stems placed in tall buckets for support as they rehydrate before being sent out to florists. The bulbs are then composted.

Smaller flower farms often find the economics of growing tulips as a cut flower challenging. Cut-and-come-again flowers such as Italian ranunculus, which produce multiple stems and can be replanted year on year, are a more viable focal flower for spring.

At home, an alternative to cutting stems is to plant tulip bulbs in pretty containers that can be brought inside for flowering. Once the flowers finish, bulbs can be planted in the garden or dry stored in a shed away from mice, ready for autumn planting.

5 Tulip taming.

Part of the tulips' charm is the unruly way the flowers flop down the side of the vase after a day or two. This is because a growth plate is located under the flower head, so the flower continues growing even when cut and in the vase.

For a more orderly effect, pop twigs or branches into the vase to support the tulip stems. Suckers from dormant fruit trees are a great candidate. When brought inside, the warmer temperature 'forces' these bare branches into life. This both elevates the arrangement and gives the tulips some support as they walk around the vase.

6 Managing tulips in warm climates.

Tulips are native to Turkey and Central Asia where winters are bitterly cold. Modern varieties still require a period of cold to thrive, so if winters are warm where you live it might be necessary to dig up your tulip bulbs when the foliage has died back. Store bulbs in a dry place, then pop into the refrigerator 6 weeks before replanting in autumn.

Alternatively, leave bulbs in the ground to perennialise (become permanent garden plants). Plant bulbs between 10 and 15 centimetres deep. This reduces the likelihood of offspring bulbils being produced, which can compromise flower quality.

Grow Me Instead

An alternative large spring flower to tulips is the easygoing Dutch iris (*Iris hollandica*), which flowers for up to 3 months in succession from late winter to mid-spring (later in cooler places). It is a great focal flower and useful in spring when long-stemmed large flowers (up to 80 centimetres) are in short supply.

The mid-blue colour is most common but it's worth hunting for the more compelling white, bicolour, burgundy and pastel blue tones. The teardrop-shaped bulbs are economically priced and will flower for many years, generously multiplying. There are two flower heads per stem; the secret to longer vase life is to gently snap off the first flower when it's finished, and the second will open. Favourite varieties include 'Discovery Sky' (pastel blue), 'Apollo' (white and yellow), 'Casablanca' (white), 'Lilac Beauty' (a dusty lilac) and 'Red Ember' (maroon).

ABOVE Tulip flat lay. Tulips are pulled with their bulbs still attached. It pays to choose your tulips wisely as stem length varies.

RIGHT Give Dutch iris a second look. They add valuable cool tones to calm vibrant spring colour schemes. The large flower size and long vase life make Dutch iris a great spring focal flower.

Recipe for a Modern Dutch Masterpiece

These still-life paintings were more than ravishing images of flowers: they were highly coded canvases, redolent with symbolism. Often, they contained vanitas – reminders of the brevity and fragility of life, represented by skulls, extinguished candles and hourglasses.

Making modern-day versions of this complicated artform is a huge amount of fun. A typical arrangement will be front facing with flowers at differing stages of life in a mass of complementary colours (those on opposite sides of the colour wheel). Flowers are at eye level sitting on a ledge or table against a dark or black background, making the illuminated subject matter glow more brightly.

This modern take on a Dutch masterpiece uses vibrant Australian and South African native flowers, in season in the warm southern hemisphere alongside spring bulbs.

Ingredients

You will need a large, heavy compote or vase, a kenzan (or flower frog), chicken wire and pot tape. And a mixture of flowers, long stemmed, short stemmed, large and small flowers, spike-shaped and trailing.

Steps

1   Begin by securing the kenzan to the base of your compote using floral putty (also known as oasis fix). Don't use too much, it can be notoriously difficult to remove.

2   Take a piece of chicken wire two to three times the area of the top of the compote. Roll and mould into a ball to fit snugly with several internal layers providing stems with maximum support. The higher the wire sits above the edge of the compote, the bigger the arrangement. Secure the chicken wire ball to the compote using pot tape.

3   Fill the compote with water. Gather your stems. Start with the tallest flowers to set the outline of the arrangement.

4   Then add the next largest flowers. These determine the focal points within the arrangement. Fill the gaps with smaller flowers, add some shorter stemmed flowers to hide the rim of the vase. Finally add in some trailing foliage.

5   Set your arrangement against a dark background and light from one side to achieve that magical Dutch masters effect.

LEFT South African and Australian native flowers give this Dutch masters-inspired arrangement a distinctive antipodean flavour.

Filler Flowers

Bulbs and More Bulbs

easy to grow • low water • cold tolerant • spring

filler • perennial • bulb • scented

Plant summary

Buy me	Plant me	I flower	Cut me
In summer and autumn. Specialist bulb growers are a great source of lesser-known varieties.	In autumn, in well-drained ground. Depth varies but a rule of thumb is to plant twice as deep as the height of the bulb.	From late winter to late spring. These spring bulbs are happiest when left alone to multiply, year after year.	Daffodils: before the flowers open but once you can see the colour of the petals. Other bulbs: when the lowest few flower buds on the stem have opened.

More Bulb Secrets

1 **Fancy daffs.**

Flowering from late winter under grey skies, adding a much-needed splash of sunshine, the humble daffodil holds a special place in gardeners' hearts. But these bright, uncomplicated 'landscape' daffodils are best left where Wordsworth found them, 'Fluttering and dancing in the breeze'. Seek out the daffodil's so-called 'fancy cousins', the double, ruffled, peachy-pink and soft lemon varieties – gorgeous when massed in earthenware jugs and hand-painted ceramic vases. Look for these fancy favourites: 'Candy Princess', 'Salou', 'My Story', 'Popeye', 'British Gamble' and 'Holland Chase'.

A relation of the daffodil, the early flowering jonquil has a beautiful form and an incredibly rich fragrance. Indoors, however, that sweet perfume can prove overpowering. Best enjoyed in the garden.

2 **The dirty dozen.**

Daffodils, ornamental kale, marigolds, cornflowers, celosia, dahlias, feverfew, snapdragons, stock, sunflowers, yarrow and zinnias dirty vase water much faster than other flowers. They release organic material, enzymes and carbohydrates as the cut stem heals. This material triggers a bacterial explosion in the vase. Here's what to do:

- After cutting, leave flowers to rehydrate in a big bucket of water in a cool place for 4 hours.

- Sear the stem ends in boiling water for 10 seconds.

- Arrange the flowers into fresh water in the vase. Remove any leaves below the water line.

LEFT Fancy daffodils are worthy of a place in your spring cutting garden. Enjoy them massed in a vase.

- Add a splash of vinegar to the vase water.

- Change the vase water every couple of days.

- Daffodils are the worst offenders and it's wisest to display them on their own rather than in a mixed bunch.

3 **Warm weather bulbs.**

Many tough but lovely bulbs hail from warmer regions. Perfect for those of us gardening in a hot climate and worth considering if your spring season is becoming warmer or you're keen to grow some unusual varieties in pots protected from the cold.

A firm Flower Farm favourite is ornithogalum (also known as chincherinchee, black pearl lily or star of Bethlehem). It has so much to recommend to florists: long, straight stems and a mass of pretty, white flowers with contrasting black or yellow centres. The flowers get longer and stronger each season, forming large clumps that can be divided every few years. Ornithogalums last 10 days in a vase and make an exceptional dried flower.

The dainty white papery flowers are robust enough to use for weddings. For a pure white effect in a bridal bouquet, pinch out the conical green tip (the remaining unopened flowers), leaving a white ball.

4 Fragrant freesias.

A South African native, freesias have been grown for cut flowers since the 1800s. They are loved for their fresh, sweet fragrance and simple beauty. Each stem bears six to ten funnel-shaped flowers opening sequentially from the base. Seek out giant freesias with longer stems reaching 40 centimetres; these make a more versatile cut flower.

Take care when cutting as the stems are very brittle. If you can find double varieties, these will be more robust and last longer as a cut flower. Plant the corms in autumn and water during spring if the weather is dry; at other times freesias require very little extra water.

Tritonia crocata are a good freesia alternative although the fragrance is not as strong. Flowering in late spring and early summer, these plants have a more upright flower spike and are equally hardy and adaptable. A variety called 'Antique Lace' is especially lovely.

5 Rethink gladdies.

Mention gladdies and the late Dame Edna's enormous brightly coloured summer bunches come to mind. A smaller, slimmer version is available in spring, in elegant pastel hues of coral, salmon and dusty pink. Each easy-to-grow corm will send up two or three spikes with as many as seven flowers per spike, and the plants' small size makes them useful for tucking into bunches. 'Blushing Bride' and 'Salmoneus' are recommended. *Gladiolus nanus* (cottage gladioli) will perennialise, flowering year after year.

LEFT Incredible ornithogalum is one of the last spring bulbs to flower.

RIGHT Right to left: Cottage gladioli 'Salmoneus', 'Las Vegas', and a regular summer flowering gladioli.

Foliage

forage • easy to grow • low water • cold tolerant • heat tolerant

spring • scented • perennial • foliage • fast growing • texture

Foliage Secrets

1 **Tough Mediterranean perennials offer brilliant foliage.**

When planning a cutting garden, it's easy to focus on flowers while forgetting the foliage. On the Flower Farm hardy Mediterranean perennials provide spring and summer foliage for bunches and vase arrangements. These plants are very vigorous and produce loads of cutting material.

Name	Variety or cultivar	Why grow it
Geranium / Pelargonium	'Oakleaf', 'Rose Geranium', 'Attar of Roses'. Geraniums are very easy to grow from cuttings so are often sold at local plant sales.	Adds lush, fresh foliage to bouquets and an incredible scent. Great grown under roses.
Olive (*Olea europaea*)	A range of varieties offer different levels of hardiness so seek local advice on what will work best in your conditions. Some varieties can even be grown as house plants.	Milky-blue, silvery, long-lasting foliage. Cut branches with green fruit for added texture. TIP: If you want an olive tree to produce fruit, don't cut the new growth but instead harvest shoots that produced fruit the previous year. Olives don't fruit on the same branch twice.
Rosemary (*Rosmarinus officinalis*)	'Salem' for tall straight stems, 'Tuscan Blue' and 'Pink Remembrance' for pretty flowers in blue and pink.	Beautiful in wreaths and as a very tough, long-lasting foliage. Use it sparingly as the scent can be overpowering. Lovely when in flower.
Ornamental oregano (*Origanum laevigatum*)	'Hopley's Purple', 'Kent Beauty' and 'Rosenkuppel'.	Long straight wands of purple, red or pink flowers over a trailing mound of fragrant, green foliage. The flowers hold their colour when dried. Good for bees.
Bay (*Laurus nobilis*)		Tough, glossy leaves and strong stems. While the bay's leaves are better known for flavouring casseroles, they can be a useful foliage plant offering leaves with a waxy sheen.
Artemisia	Prairie sage (*Artemisia ludoviciana*) and wormwood (*Artemisia absinthium*)	The silver, lacy foliage is lovely in bunches but don't cut until stems are woody (younger stems will wilt). Artemisia adds the most wonderful white highlights to fresh and dried arrangements.

LEFT Flat leafed parsley, gone to seed, makes a great cut foliage, adding texture, airiness and a spring freshness to arrangements.

2 **Herbs running to seed make great foliage.**

Who hasn't wandered out to the vegetable patch to cut parsley or coriander only to discover the herb running to seed. One minute you have a culinary staple, the next – tall, airy flower heads dancing in the breeze. It seems to happen overnight. But these dainty stems are perfect as scented foliage or filler in bunches. Also consider fennel, basil and mint (apple mint, pineapple mint, lemon bergamot).

3 **Beware of floppy foliage.**

It's very tempting to harvest the first bright, fresh green foliage of spring. Before you head out to cut armfuls, test for rigidity by popping a couple of stems in a vase to see how they hold up. Immature foliage is prone to drooping because of an absence of woody lignin in the stem. If foliage flops in the vase, wait a few weeks then try again. Sometimes much of the stem is sturdy, but the immature tips still droop – simply snip these off. This 'tip pruning' is often necessary for eucalyptus and olive branches even later in the season.

4 **Foliage can change the 'personality' of a bouquet.**

Far from simply bulking up a bunch, foliage provides a wonderful backdrop for flowers and, depending on the leaf colour, shape, size, shine and texture, can alter the personality of an arrangement. When thinking about the mood you want your flowers to evoke – happy, celebratory, soothing, calming or relaxing – carefully choose your foliage.

RIGHT A freshly cut spring bouquet of stock, Dutch iris, aquilegia, Mount Morgan wattle and delphinium.

Airy Elements and Texture

easy to grow • low water • perennial • spring • heat tolerant • bulb • airy

Dancing Spring Secrets

1 Unusual bulbs to add texture or airy lightness.

Peacock iris (*Moraea aristata*): Critically endangered in the wild in its native South Africa, this is a most beautiful little flower. Borne on fine, wiry stems, crisp white petals are adorned with an iridescent blue eye, rather like a peacock feather. Despite their exotic appearance, peacock irises are very easy to grow and best left in the ground to naturalise. Flowering winter into spring. Stunning in delicate table arrangements where the flowers can be admired in detail.

Queen Fabiola (*Tritelleia iaxa*): Flowering late spring to early summer, this is a great bulb for poor soils and comes into its own just as other spring bulbs are fading. Bees and butterflies love the mass of purple flowers, and as a cut flower with a shorter stem it looks lovely in a bud vase, lasting about a week. Wonderful paired with soft pink and peach roses.

African corn lily (*Ixia hybrida*): This South African lily dances above bouquets with tall arching stems, fine grassy foliage and star-like flowers. The flowers come in a range of colours, each with a dark centre. They are especially useful, flowering during a lean time in the garden, bridging the gap between the spring flowering bulbs and summer perennials. Flowers last up to 2 weeks in a vase. As they are slender plants, they look best in the garden when planted in groups. Sparaxis is similar to ixia and they work well together.

2 Cloud dreaming with larkspurs.

Larkspurs are an annual form of delphinium. The most common variety is *Delphinium chinensis*, also a great cut flower, but take a moment to discover *Consolida regalis*. This bushier plant has a similar effect to baby's breath (gypsophila) in a bunch. A mass of tiny flowers forms a cloud and looks captivating alone or when dancing above a bunch of other stems. Easy to grow from seed. Search for 'Blue Cloud' and 'White Cloud' cultivars.

TIP: Sear stem ends in hot water

A favourite trick of florists, searing stem ends in boiling water extends vase life. Searing increases the surface area for water absorption and forces out any air bubbles in the stem. This allows water to be readily drawn up the stem, enabling the plant to drink, the cells to remain turgid, and the petals to be hydrated and full. Not unlike searing your home-grown peas in boiling water before cooling in cold water and freezing for eating later. Except for daffodils, plants grown from bulbs do not need to be seared. But most stems benefit if you can spare the time. The searing duration is linked to the woodiness of the stem:

- Sear super-delicate fleshy stems for 5 seconds.
- Sear mid-thickness stems such as cosmos and ammi for 10 seconds.
- Sear roses and other woody shrubs for 20 seconds.
- Sear blossom branches and big natives including proteas for 30 seconds.

To sear stems:

- Place the bottom 2–3 centimetres of the stem in water that has just come off the boil with the flower angled away from the steam.
- Immediately plunge the stem into cold water.

Four seasons of flowers

Summer.

The Secret to Summer Success

On the Flower Farm, the arrival of summer sometimes overlaps with late spring making it one of the more weather-sensitive times of the year. While in cooler climates there is generally an orderly parade of new plants coming into flower, a freak hot week in a warm climate can result in spring and summer flowers appearing all at once. It makes planning a little tricky but keeps everyone on their toes with no two years ever proving exactly the same. During normal seasons, the Flower Farm relies heavily on hardworking biennials including Canterbury bells, chocolate lace flower and dianthus to plug the gap between spring and summer and provide a continuous flow of flowers.

A summer cutting garden overflowing with flowers is the stuff of dreams and a thousand gardening books. These images sustain us through the cold winter months and the manic planting and weeding of spring. By the time the sun is high in the sky and mercury rising, we're ready to enjoy the fruits of our labour.

The secret to a successful cutting garden over summer, especially in warm and unpredictable climates, is prioritising heat-loving, low-water-use plants, organising watering systems and harvesting rainwater, mulching to reduce water loss, and rising with the birds to cut those precious summer flowers.

We can retreat indoors during the heat of the day. Plants are not so lucky. Choose varieties that thrive rather than merely survive in the heat. A plant that is happy with the prevailing conditions will produce healthier, larger, more beautiful flowers that last longer in the vase. It makes sense to prioritise heat lovers in the summer cutting garden. And you'd be surprised at just how many pretty cut flowers fit the bill. There's even a heat-loving foxglove.

Fill your summer vases with delicately scented roses, wild sweet peas, tall delphiniums and bicoloured snapdragons. Perennials from the Mediterranean bring filler flowers in soft white, pink and blue hues. A few short weeks later these flowers will be joined by North American prairie plants in confident rich gold, bronze, burgundy and mustard, signalling the approach of autumn and a change in colour palette.

LEFT Elevate a beach party with rustic ceramic vases filled with grasses and sea holly. Add a little freshness with sprigs of feverfew in milk bottles. Heavy-bottomed containers will work best and stand up to wayward gusts of wind.

RIGHT Sunflowers add a pop of colour to the biscuit tones of the Australian summer landscape.

Hero Flower

Roses

CCA • long flowering • easy to grow • round • heat tolerant • focal

cup shaped • cold tolerant • summer • dried • scented • perennial

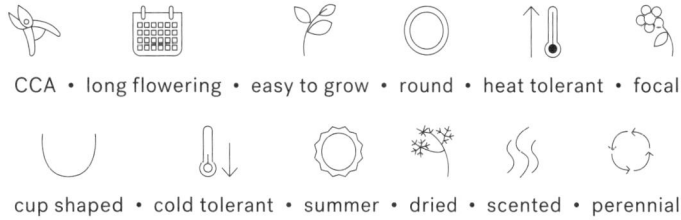

Plant summary

Buy me	Plant me	I flower	Cut me
As bare-rooted plants. Shipped in winter when dormant. If possible, pre-order in summer or early autumn to secure the prettiest colours.	Seek local advice regarding your prevailing conditions. As a rule of thumb bare-rooted roses are planted in winter in warm climates and early spring in colder climates.	From mid-spring (warm climates) or early summer (cooler climates) to autumn. More recent breeding has developed varieties that bloom almost continuously or provide multiple flushes of flowers throughout the season.	Long stems at marshmallow stage (see p. 94). Once cut, immediately plunge stem into a bucket of cool water.

Secrets of the Rose

1 **Garden roses are back.**

In the recent past, this most eulogised of blooms fell out of favour as a cut flower. Consumers became disheartened by the sad, scentless hothouse roses imported from Kenya, South America and other faraway places. Tight, cone-shaped blooms, these flowers sulked and stubbornly refused to open. But spare a thought for the stems' difficult life journey, subjected to multiple chemical baths to satisfy strict import requirements, dehydrated and rehydrated so many times while being transported that the flowers were ostensibly dead. Hardly surprising that people began asking florists for 'anything but roses'. Even brides were shying away from this wedding day staple.

Then, suddenly, social media was awash with images of florists 'reflexing' roses (see p. 97). This laborious process involves bending back petals one by one, opening the flower up and creating the effect of a larger, home-grown garden rose. At the time, very few garden roses were available to florists.

Before long, savvy growers realised that garden roses looked even better than reflexed roses and could be grown locally. Zero airmiles and much better fragrance. Boutique field-grown rose farms soon sprang up across the US with American brides carrying big, ruffled long-stemmed bridal bouquets. With the dusty, muddy tones of 'Honey Dijon', 'Soul Sister' and 'Koko Loko' trending at weddings, it was clear floristry was heading for a serious rose revival.

LEFT Floribunda type roses are a Flower Farm favourite. Snip out the earliest flowers that have gone over and you've still got plenty to enjoy.

2 Grow modern varieties for cutting.

Old roses are a treasured part of our gardening memory. However, many of these varieties produce spindly, short flower stems borne on a fiercely thorny bush. That's why our grandmothers kept tiny crystal bud vases stashed in the cupboard, perfect for those short stems. We still love our old-fashioned roses, but if you're growing for cut flowers, then long, strong stems and a disease-resistant plant are crucial.

The secret to wonderful cut stems is to plant a rose bush with these characteristics:

- Recently, rose breeders have prioritised disease resistance and a tolerance for prevailing climatic conditions (your local rose grower will be best to advise you).

- Hybrid tea or floribunda (spray) type.

- Bush habit (not a climber or standard).

- High petal count for longer vase life; open-centre varieties are pollinated quickly thereby reducing the vase life. However, avoid very densely petalled cup-shaped forms as these can become waterlogged and may rot.

- Repeat or continuous flowering.

- Thorn-free or minimal thorns.

- Vigorous and producing long, straight stems. Bigger, taller plants are more likely to produce stems long enough for the vase.

- Scented. Perfume will set your roses apart from the imported hothouse varieties that have scent bred out to extend vase life. We like to visit specialist rose growers in the summer when plants are flowering so we can select for fragrance as well as colour. The descriptors are incredibly enticing: old rose, tea, myrrh, musk and fruity.

3 Prune hard for the best stems.

Once bare-root roses are well established (typically a couple of years), it's important to keep to a strict maintenance calendar. Having said that, roses are among the lowest maintenance plants you can grow – tough, waterwise and incredibly giving. Pruning is the biggest job and sometimes a prickly task. Long sleeves and good gloves are recommended. For the best roses:

- Prune in mid-winter (warm climate) or late winter to early spring (cool climate) when the bushes are dormant. After cutting back the foliage so the inside of the plant is visible, prune out crossing, dead or damaged stems. Next, cut out stems in the centre of the plant to improve airflow and achieve an open-vase shape. Make your pruning cuts just above an outward facing bud. We aim for low bushes of five to nine stems at about 40 centimetres high. Pop the cuttings straight into a tub to avoid double handling the thorny stems.

- Once leaves appear and are growing, fertilise with an organic slow-release fertiliser in spring and again in late summer (after the first big flush of flowers).

- Mulch after fertilising in spring to help retain moisture and suppress weeds.

- Do a light summer prune to get a second flush.

Not much work for months of gorgeous flowers!

OPPOSITE Roses grown for different purposes, clockwise from top left: large, scented flowers for wedding arbours; delicate wild-style roses for little milk bottles; tropical tones for happy birthday bunches; candy pink for classic cottage garden arrangements.

4 **Cut long and low.**

When rose stems are cut for the vase, this is a form of pruning. Cut 'long and low' just above a bud or pair of leaves, taking almost the whole length of the stem. This encourages the plant to produce more long, straight stems. If a flower is not cut for the vase and has gone over, don't deadhead in the traditional way by snipping just under the flower head. Cut the stem long and low to discourage spindly stems.

5 **Roses love company.**

Good riddance to the traditional and drearily municipal 'rose bed' featuring nothing but roses, emerging from a sea of mulch. Such a waste of space when, instead, you can intersperse those roses with pretty Mediterranean perennial shrubs like salvias, geranium and achillea. These plants help manage pests and diseases, cool the roses' root zone and provide handy bouquet ingredients. Select dwarf varieties to ensure good air circulation around the rose bushes. Salvia is helpful in managing blackspot on rose leaves, the plants exuding sulphuric compounds that act as a natural fungicide.

You can also extend the season by underplanting roses with early flowering spring bulbs or interplanting with heirloom chrysanthemums to flower after the roses have almost finished.

6 **When to cut?**
The sepals secret.

Cut an immature flower and it may never fully open. Conversely an open flower that has already been visited by the bees and pollinated can drop petals or bend at the neck a few hours after cutting.

For good vase life, concentrate on the sepals at the base of the flower rather than the petals. When two-thirds of these sepals are reflexed back and the flower is at the 'marshmallow' stage (give it a little squeeze), the flower is ready for cutting.

On the Flower Farm, if we need lots of beautiful open roses for a wedding or event, we harvest at the 'marshmallow' stage and store the flowers indoors in buckets for between 3 and 5 days (with a daily water change). In our bee-free studio the flowers are safe from pollinators, insects and damage from wind and rain. Here the roses open gradually, filling the space with a gorgeous fragrance. One of the perks of the job.

Favourite roses
for cutting

- 'Gertrude Jekyll'
- 'Novalis'
- 'Francis Meilland'
- 'Soul Sister'
- 'Tineke'
- 'Just Joey'

OPPOSITE First flush on the Flower Farm.

Planting Bare-root Roses

Roses are sold either growing in pots with visible green leaves or as dormant bare-root plants with just a bag covering the roots to keep them moist. Don't be alarmed by the plant's twiggy, lifeless appearance – lush colour and fragrance lurk within.

Sourcing roses as bare-root plants has many advantages:

- There is a wider variety to choose from, and plants are released earlier in the season. The sooner the roses are in the ground, the sooner they start to establish good root systems – before the weather warms and their water needs increase.

- It is unsustainable to freight plants in heavy pots. Lightweight bare-root roses are a more ecological and economical choice.

For warm climates plant bare-root roses in winter. In cooler climates hold off until spring if the ground is frozen or waterlogged.

However, if you live in a very cold climate, potted roses might be a better alternative for spring planting. Contact a specialist rose grower for their advice and source your plants locally.

- Unwrap and, weather permitting, plant your bare-root roses the moment they arrive.

- Soak the roots in a bucket of water for up to 4 hours to rehydrate.

- Prune back roots by around a third.

- Dig a hole as deep and twice as wide as the plant.

- Fill the hole with water to hydrate the ground and allow it to drain away to check the soil is free draining.

- Dip the roots in mycorrhizal powder to assist with root development.

- Using some of the soil you have removed build a little cone-shaped mound in the middle of the hole to support the roots. Rest the plant on top of the cone and fan out the roots (this will also enhance drainage) then backfill, ensuring that the graft union (where the plant is attached to the root stock) sits just above soil level. Firm down.

- Trim back the top growth of the rose by a third.

- Water in well to allow the soil to settle.

It's crucial that roses are well watered in the first year, especially in hot weather, until the plants develop more extensive root systems. Feed new roses with a seaweed foliar spray. After the first year add organic granular fertiliser (no sooner as it may burn the rose's new roots). During the first year, prune buds before the flower develops so the plant directs energy into root formation. This will provide a stronger plant and by year three the rose will be pumping out long flower stems.

ABOVE If your established garden roses have short stems, snip a few and enjoy them in little vases.

<u>How to</u>

Reflex a Rose

1 Choose flowers that are two-thirds open with pliable petals.

2 Blow strongly into the centre of the flower to loosen the petals.

3 Hold the flower upside down and gently twist the stem between your palms shaking off any water and encouraging the internal petals to open.

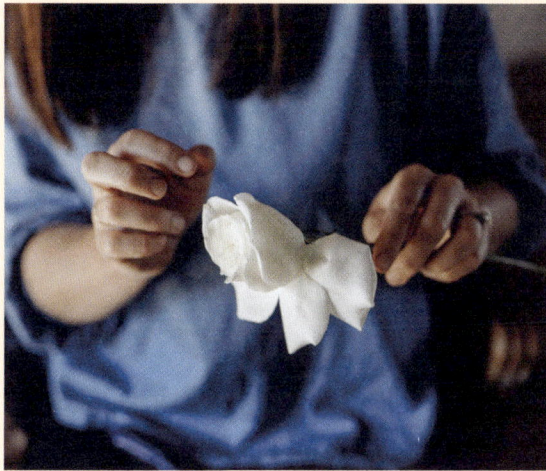

4 With the rose upright again, remove the guard petals on the outside of the rose, snapping off at the base of the flower (leave the sepals). These petals are designed to protect the rose and are slightly wavy and thicker in texture and often a different colour.

5 Starting from the outside of the rose, carefully fold the petals back and down, working around the flower. Place your thumb at the base of the petal and 'stroke' it back and over your thumb.

6 Reflex approximately two to three layers. Don't open the whole rose. Blow again on the internal petals to loosen them slightly.

7 Spray the heads of the reflexed roses with a fine mist of water (from around a metre above the flowers) to keep the blooms fresh and hydrated.

8 Recut the stems at a 45-degree angle and place back into water.

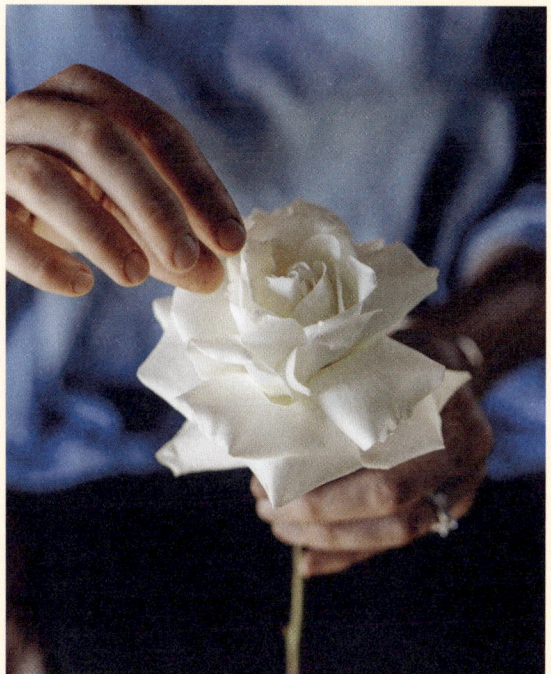

Grow Me Instead

Lisianthus

If you don't have the space to grow roses or are renting and don't want to invest in costly perennials, lisianthus is a great warm climate alternative, flowering when other soft petaled blooms are in short supply. The foliage is juicy and slightly milky coloured, making it a soft and elegant addition to bunches.

When planted into cool soil in late winter to mid-spring (depending on your climate), the plants will flush twice and are perennial in warmer climates; however, the best flowering is in the first year, so most growers tend to replant annually. Once lisianthus has put down deep roots, the plant will take whatever summer throws at it. This Texan native just loves baking under a hot sun. There are two secrets to success with lisianthus:

Grow from plugs or small plants

Don't bother growing from seed. Lisianthus takes a mind-numbing 10 to 12 weeks to grow a few sets of leaves during which time it requires consistently perfect conditions. Source seedlings or small plants from your local flower farmer.

In warm climates, plant out in autumn. The seedlings will overwinter in well-drained soil. If you have heavier clay soils or live in a cooler climate (equivalent to US zone 7 or cooler) plant out when the soil has defrosted in spring.

Plant in cool weather

This prevents a condition called rosetting. This can happen if seedlings are planted when the weather is too warm and before plants have established a decent root system. To survive these inhospitable conditions, the plants fall dormant. This can be a tricky problem to reverse so avoid it altogether and plant before the weather gets too warm. Keep the plants well weeded and well watered and plant closely together (10 centimetres x 10 centimetres) so as the sun gets stronger, the foliage shades the root zone. This super-tight spacing helps the plants support each other and encourages the plants to grow taller.

Cool-toned plants

There's something timeless about the pairing of blue or purple perennials with warm-toned roses. For a true country garden aesthetic, try:

- *Verbena bonariensis*
- Globe thistle (*Echinops ritro* 'Veitch's Blue')
- *Allium hollandicum* 'Purple Sensation'
- English lavender (*Lavandula angustifolia* 'Hidcote')
- *Ageratum houstonianum*
- *Salvia farinacea* 'Blue Bedder Sage'

RIGHT A wonderful alternative to roses, the lisianthus adds a soft, sophisticated note to bunches.

BELOW Lisianthus planted closely together for a shaded root zone and strong, healthy plants.

Roses and a Changing Climate

Recently, the celebrated English growing company, David Austin, discontinued some of their most popular roses because the plants were no longer performing in changing weather conditions globally. This was a shock to many rose lovers but underscores the importance of considering more recently bred varieties.

Diseases and pests have evolved, and climates are changing. As a result, some Austin favourites including 'A Shropshire Lad' and 'Munstead Wood' are no longer viable. A healthy rose is a beautiful rose, a plant ravaged by pests or covered in blackspot is not.

In a sobering move, plant breeders are now prioritising climate resistance over scent and showy blooms. Trial breeding is being undertaken in several countries – those with arid climates as well as those with humid conditions and heavy, sustained rain events – to test how the roses will perform in future decades. Breeders hope these new varieties, which contain genes from wild roses with higher disease resistance, will provide good flowers whatever weather comes our way.

Damp conditions create the perfect breeding ground for blackspot and powdery mildew. Summer rain events and rising humidity can strongly impact old roses that haven't been bred for such conditions, making the plants more susceptible to disease. Some rose growers in the US have started to categorise their roses by climatic zone, and hopefully this model will be widely adopted by rose breeders in the future.

LEFT Abandoned rusty farm vehicles were brought back to life and flower-bombed during a time of excess on the Flower Farm. A sheet of mesh was laid in the open tray (higher at the front and lower at the back) to hold the stems of roses, linaria, Canterbury bells, sweet William, watsonia 'Lilac Towers', veronica and delphinium.

THIS PAGE When planning colour schemes for large events, we cut a selection to see how the flowers work together. This is especially important when using roses, given the incredible range of shades and hues.

Focal Flowers

Lilies

bulb • heat tolerant • summer • perennial • scented

easy to grow • focal • trumpet shape • long vase life

Plant summary

Buy me	Plant me	I flower	Cut me
As dormant bulbs. Varieties best for cut flowers include Oriental, Asiatic, LA hybrids and Tiger hybrids.	In early spring in a sunny spot. Plant 10 to 20 cm deep and 20 to 30 cm apart into ground that is well drained over winter. Mulch once green growth is visible. Lift and divide bulb clumps every 3 to 4 years as lily bulbs multiply beautifully.	From late spring to late summer. If dry weather occurs in the month before flowering, water regularly for longer stems.	Before flowers open (the petals bruise very easily). Flower buds should be swollen but the colour of the petals not yet visible.

Long Lived Secrets

1 **Shapely flowers.**

The trumpet flower shape is among the least common in the gardening world but one of the most impressive. And lilies (*Lilium*) are the best of the best: big, lush, long-lasting and heat tolerant.

Lilies make brilliant cut flowers whether you live in a warm or chilly place. They repeat flower year after year, requiring little other than a well-drained spot and a bit of extra water and fertiliser during the growing season. Plants fall dormant after flowering only to return the following year with even bigger blooms on tall, sturdy stems up to a metre and a half tall (depending on variety).

Lilies are a fantastically long-lived cut flower, lasting 2 to 3 weeks in the vase. As the flowers fade, the dried seed pods make rustic additions to dried flower arrangements. Breeding in recent years has developed double varieties and pollen- and scent-free cultivars. Good news for allergy sufferers.

LEFT Lilies have upward, downward and sideways facing flower heads. Upward is most useful for arranging but there's something charming about the shape and behaviour of the shy downward facing flowers.

2 **Keeping lilies in bloom.**

The secret to ensuring healthy lilies year on year, while still cutting flowers for the vase, is to leave half of the plant's stalk attached to the bulb. Ensure sufficient leaves remain for photosynthesis to continue and for reserves to be directed back into the bulb for good flowers the following year. Choosing tall varieties will make this much easier.

3 **Staggered planting.**

To enjoy months of flowers, grow a mixture of early and late flowering types. Early varieties include Asiatic, Tango and Tiger; late varieties include Oriental and Oriental Trumpet. Or hold newly purchased bulbs in an old fridge where food isn't stored (every part of the lily plant is poisonous) and plant in batches over several months to extend the flowering window.

Cutting garden favourites

- 'Tiger Babies'
- 'White Twinkle'
- 'Red Velvet'
- 'Pink Giant'
- Doubles 'Must See' and 'Broken Heart'

RIGHT Pollen-free lilies including 'Easy Whisper' and 'Easy Dance', and upward facing Tango lilies 'Pieton', 'Cogoleto' and 'Purple Eye'.

Grow Me Instead

Pineapple Lily

Although called a lily, this plant is not a member of the *Lilium* family. Rather, it hails from South Africa and is drought-tolerant and easy to grow. Flowering for a long period over summer and autumn, the plants are as beguiling in the garden as in the vase. Cut stems last a staggering month with water changes.

The flowering stalk is speckled with star-shaped flowers in shades from pink to white and green. *Eucomis comosa* 'Sparkling Burgundy' is especially lovely. Plant the dormant bulbs in winter or spring in a well-drained spot as they are liable to rot if the ground is too wet. In a full sun position, they will become a permanent feature of your garden.

Tuberose

There is possibly no more intoxicating flower scent, reminiscent of orange blossom or ylang-ylang. Pure white star-like flowers are borne on tall stems from late summer into autumn, when many of our most popular seasonal flowers – dahlias, chrysanthemums and rudbeckias – are without fragrance.

Native to Mexico, the tuberose is ideally suited to warmer gardens and likes a sunny spot. Plant the clump-forming rhizomes in late winter to early spring after the danger of frost has passed, with just the tip of the bulb showing at the surface. Keep moist during the growing period. They multiply easily and can remain in the ground in many areas. If you have heavy frosts, lift in late autumn and store somewhere dry over winter.

Trumpet-shaped alternatives

These flowers have a similar aesthetic to trumpet-shaped lilies in a bouquet and make a good substitute at different points in the year:

- Peruvian lily (*Alstromeria*). Sends up a steady stream of stems from spring to autumn. Exceptionally tough with long-lasting flowers. We love the mustard and dusky pink tones of 'Butterscotch'.

- Gladioli (*Gladiolus*). The very long stems are suited to large summer arrangements. Coral is a most useful tone, but when creating arrangements for a celebration it's hard to resist a mix of neon, clashing colours.

- Bearded iris (*Iris* x *germanica*). Fragrant bicolour flowers in a vast array of combinations. From muddy browns and lilacs, and pinks to butter yellow, you'll have trouble choosing. Do remember to plant rhizomes in a sunny, well-drained spot. Varieties flower from early spring to early autumn.

TOP Incredible pineapple lily adds drama to arrangements.

ABOVE Alstromeria are a heat-loving, hardworking, plant-and-forget member of the Flower Farm. We cut stems for 6 months of the year.

RIGHT A sunny mixture of sunflowers, rudbeckia, alstromeria, calendula and kangaroo paw.

BELOW Single-stem varieties are closely planted for smaller flower heads and slender stems.

Sunflowers

Did you know that there are two types of sunflowers – branching and single stemmed? The secret to deciding which to grow has everything to do with pollen and vase life.

Single-stem varieties

Sunflowers stocked by your local florist will normally be single-stem varieties. Just one flower per plant, but a flower that will last up to 2 weeks in the vase. The flowers don't produce pollen (so no messy tablecloths), although they do produce nectar so are still visited by the bees. Single stem varieties don't generally produce seeds although sometimes pollinators may bring pollen from other sunflowers, and the occasional seed may develop.

Single-stem sunflowers (like the ProCut and Sunrich series or 'Vincent's Choice') are quick to mature, taking from 50 to 80 days depending on the variety. To ensure the flowers don't grow too large to be added to mixed bunches and arrangements, plant seeds close together. Space at 10 centimetres x 10 centimetres for smaller flowers in mixed bouquets or at 15 centimetres x 15 centimetres for bigger stems in straight sunflower bunches. Handy for small gardens.

Branching varieties

Branching varieties come in incredible colours of burgundy, chocolate, amber, bronze and bicolour. 'Autumn Beauty', 'Strawberry Blonde' and 'Soraya' are recommended, but our kitchen table favourites are the double-flowered varieties such as 'Teddy Bear'.

Space these large plants at least 45 centimetres apart. They produce numerous flowers over a long period throughout the summer. The first cut stems will always be the best and strongest and can be used as focal flowers. The remaining side stems are best as filler flowers, though shorter side stems at strange angles can be a challenge for flower arranging. And unlike single-stem sunflowers, branching varieties do produce pollen. This is wonderful for future seed saving – but not great for tablecloths or vase life. As soon as the flower is pollinated, it starts to go over. Harvest flowers when the petals are just visible and expect around 5 to 7 days vase life.

Careful planning at the beginning of the season will provide sunflowers throughout summer and autumn. Sow the first batch under cover in early spring. Then direct sow as often as every 2 weeks, depending on space. On the Flower Farm, two varieties are sown at a time, with colours changing as the season progresses.

In late spring to early summer, light, bright lemon and soft colours work well with late spring bulbs and pastel bunches. The classic sunflower yellow stands up to the bright UV light of high summer. Come autumn, we're craving more rusty tones, burnt oranges and mustards.

TOP Single-stem sunflowers in manageable sizes for a vase arrangement.

ABOVE Our fluffy favourite sunflower – Teddy Bear.

Filler Flowers

Perennials

easy to grow • low water • summer • scented • perennial • long flowering • filler

heat tolerant • cold tolerant • herbs • airy • daisy • line/spike • globe • texture

Summer's abundance provides an almost overwhelming selection of potential filler flowers to plump up bouquets and load arrangements. Filter by colour, flower shape, and heat and drought tolerance when choosing what to grow.

Perennial Secrets

1 Look to the Mediterranean for soft pastel tones.

The Mediterranean can be hot and dry with poor soil, all good indicators for selecting plants that thrive in challenging summer conditions. Many plants from this beautiful part of the world are deeply fragrant, such as rosemary, thyme, sage and bay. And flowers tend to be dainty in soft blues, pinks, purples and whites including lavender, salvias, nepeta, jasmine and cistus.

One of the most useful space fillers in a bunch is yarrow (*Achillea millefolium*). Chalky flat-head flowers sit atop frilly aromatic leaves and come in many colours: pastels, mixed berry tones, cotton white and rich oranges. We love 'Colorado', 'Summer Berries', 'Summer Pastels' and 'The Pearl'.

2 Look to the North American prairies for rich, bold tones.

In shades of burnt orange, yellow, red and magenta, the prairie plants of North America flower from mid-summer into autumn when sunset tones are most desirable. These flowers team effortlessly with dahlias, zinnias and sunflowers, providing textural elements, movement and lightness to focal flowers that might otherwise seem a little heavy.

Rudbeckias are one of the best prairie plants for cutting. Look for *Rudbeckia hirta*, compact plants that are best for petite arrangements and the colours are incredible. *Rudbeckia triloba* is better for cold climates; it is hardier, taller and comes in classic colours of yellow and gold. Other excellent rudbeckias for cutting:

- 'Cherry Brandy' in red wine tones.

- 'Sahara'. Semi-double and double flowers in caramel, copper and warm pink tones.

- 'Prairie Sun'. Green centre with gold petals, tipped in lemon.

- 'Indian Summer'. The classic rudbeckia: black centre with gold petals.

LEFT Low-maintenance perennials are great companions for focal roses and dahlias. Here abelia, veronica, *Caryopteris incana*, pineapple lily, lemon verbena, *Salvia leucantha* and astrantia fill vases on an old Welsh dresser.

One peculiarity of rudbeckias is that from time to time newly formed flowers wilt when first harvested. 'Indian Summer' is particularly prone to this pesky behaviour. Give cut stems a big drink for 24 hours and double check before adding to a bouquet. More mature blooms will be firmer at harvest.

Echinacea is another strong cut flower candidate and looks like rudbeckia; both are called coneflowers. Gently touch the flower's central cone. If the cone is spiky, it's an echinacea, if smooth, it's a rudbeckia.

3 Know your onions.

Alliums are members of the onion family. The globe-like flowers make brilliant cut stems – from 10 days to 3 weeks vase life – and excellent dried flowers. Make the most of flowering vegetable crops like onions, garlic, shallots and leeks or grow ornamental varieties in your cutting garden. When harvesting:

- Cut the stem and immediately place in a bucket of water; the onion smell will dissipate after a few hours.

- Arrange in a vase of fresh water and change the water regularly.

- Grow a range of varieties for different flower sizes. Some of the best ornamental varieties are 'Star of Persia' (*Allium christophii*), 'Drumstick Allium' (*Allium atropurpureum*), 'Sicilian Honey Garlic' (*Allium bulgaricum siculum*), 'White Garlic' (*Allium cowanii*), *Allium elatum*, Ornamental Onion (*Allium* 'Firmament').

ABOVE Rudbeckias are highly valued in the late-summer cutting garden.

ABOVE Smaller allium flowers from the vegetable garden can also be woven into arrangements.

RIGHT The metre-long stems of allium 'Purple Rain'. Harvest for the purple star-shaped flowers or wait for the heavy seed heads.

4 Grow snapdragons for height in arrangements.

Spike or line flowers give an arrangement height and are crucial to floristry, and one of the Flower Farm's favourites is the pretty snapdragon. This tough plant flowers for much of the year in temperate conditions but less over winter in cool climates and less over summer in very hot climates. In addition to the classic snapdragon flower shape, beautiful open-faced varieties such as 'Chantilly' or 'Madame Butterfly' are available in beguiling colours and worth searching for.

Although perennial, snapdragons are normally treated as an annual because the plants aren't as vigorous after the first season and are prone to rust. Replant in a different location each year. Otherwise, they are easy to grow:

- Sow the dust-like seed onto a seed tray. Once the plants are big enough to handle, prick out the seedlings and plant into little pots. Harden off and plant outside when each plant has a few sets of leaves.

- Snapdragons are sensitive to day-length, light intensity and temperature. While most seed sold for home gardeners is for spring or summer flowers, commercially grown varieties are divided into numbered groups according to their season of flowering. If your seed has a number in the title, search online to make sure it matches the time of year you need the flowers.

Grow your snapdragons 15 centimetres x 15 centimetres apart. This allows the plants to support each other in windy weather, but also provides enough space for side shoots to branch out. Be sure to use Hortonova netting or stakes to support plants.

Snapdragons are geotropic plants, meaning they grow against gravity. If a plant falls over, the flower head will turn to face upright, and you will never be able to correct that drunken kink. For this reason, immediately place cut flowers into a high-sided bucket to ensure stems remain straight.

ABOVE 'Appleblossom' snapdragon.

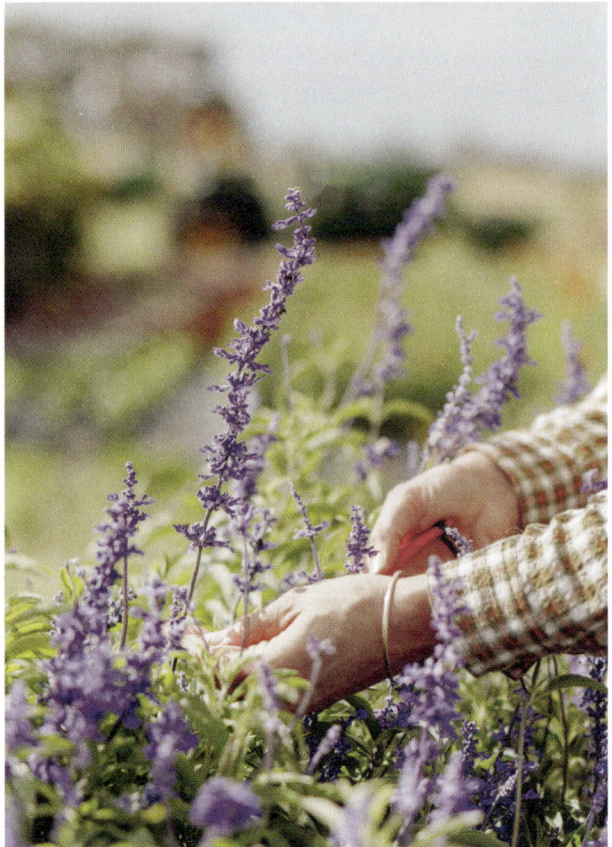

Grow Me Instead

Try these spike-shaped alternatives to snapdragons:

- Delphiniums (perennial) or larkspur (annual). Grown especially for the range of blue and purple tones not found in snapdragons. The Flower Farm's favourite is the gorgeous 'Magic Fountains Sky Blue White Bee'. 'Belladonna Mix' is the hardiest, most cold-tolerant variety.

- Classic foxgloves (*Digitalis purpurea*). If you live in a warm climate, seek out the 'Café Crème' foxglove (*Digitalis lanata*) which flowers later and is more heat- and drought-tolerant – a woolly plant originating from Greece and the hotter parts of eastern Europe. Pearl, coffee-brown and gold flowers are smaller but mass together beautifully to give a soft, earthy effect.

- Digiplexis is a result of breeding between the hardy foxglove (*Digitalis*) and *Isoplexis canariensis*, a rare plant from the Canary Islands. Digiplexis perennialise and flower for up to 6 months a year from late spring to autumn. They are fully frost hardy and drought-tolerant, so make a great choice in many climates. We particularly love 'Foxlight Ruby Glow'.

- Veronica. The 'Skyler' series is best for cutting.

- Verbascum. An incredible family of plants and we'd love to grow them all; the 'Southern Charm' mix is most useful, and its dusky tones are hard to resist.

- Lupins (*Lupinus*). The Russell mix offers a range of colours.

Salvia – the sage family

A mixture of annual, biennial and perennial forms, salvias hail from multiple geographies including the Mediterranean and North America. The hardy varieties are best for cutting. In particular:

- Mexican bush sage (*Salvia leucantha*). Velvety flowers in white, pink and purple.

- Clary sage (*Salvia sclarea*). Easy to grow from seed with flowers in white, pink, purple and blue. While unremarkable on the plant, the straight stems topped with coloured bracts are long lasting and surprisingly effective in bouquets. Choose a mix or go for the single colours 'Blue Monday' or 'Pink Sunday'.

- 'Blue Bedder' (*Salvia farinacea*). Silvery blue flowers and healthy green leaves are amazing in arrangements, resembling lavender.

- 'Fairy Queen' (*Salvia farinacea*). Pretty blue and white flowers from early summer until winter.

- 'Bog Sage' (*Salvia uliginosa*). Spikes of perfect sky-blue flowers, quite unlike the colour of anything else on the Flower Farm.

CLOCKWISE FROM TOP LEFT
Delphiniums; Café Crème foxgloves; 'Blue Bedder' salvia; digiplexis.

Mediterranean Perennials

These varieties of Mediterranean perennials are valuable filler flowers.

Name	Variety or cultivar	Features
Lavender (*Lavandula*)	'Grosso', 'Edelweiss', 'Impress Purple', 'Canary Island Lavender'	Scented, soft, milky foliage with an iconic flower head. Great for drying but deserves to be used more as a fresh cut flower.
Sea holly (*Eryngium planum* or *E. giganteum*)	'Blue Glitter', 'White Glitter', 'Miss Willmott's Ghost', 'Deep Blue'	Adds a splash of blue and the textural addition is amazing. Great with roses. Long lasting. Dried flower.
Echinops	'Ritro Blue', 'Star Frost', and 'Veitch's Blue'	As useful as sea holly but with a pleasing golf ball shape. Extra-long lasting and an excellent dried flower.
Aster	Easter daisy ('Ruby Buttons'), New York aster (*Symphyotrichom novi-belgii*), Stokes' aster (*Stokesia laevis*)	Exceptionally long vase life, long summer/autumn flowering window and wonderful for bringing a bunch of stems together.

North American Prairie Perennials

Drought-tolerant once established, these lesser-known perennials do well in a forgotten sunny corner of the garden and make fine cut flowers. Treat these plants as annuals if you live in a colder climate:

Name	Variety or cultivar	Features
Echinacea purpurea	'White Swan', 'Prima Donna Deep Rose', 'PowWow Wild Berry', 'Magnus', 'Green Twister'	The original clashing pink and orange flowers create a dynamic neon bouquet. For a calmer look, grow white, pink, rose and lemon/green tones.
Anise hyssop (*Agastache foeniculum*)	'Golden Jubilee'	Cools down hot-toned summer flowers like rudbeckias and sunflowers in a lively market bunch. Great for drying. Smells of anise.
Dense blazing star (*Liatris spicata*)	'Floristan Violet', 'Floristan White'	Numerous, long, wand-like spikes densely set with white or violet-coloured flowers. Drops florets, so use for events only.
Penstemon barbatus	'Husker Red'	Handy, long flowering window. Continues flowering when little else is around.
Floss flower (*Ageratum houstonianum*)	Wild form	Perennial in warm climates and provides an almost constant supply of valuable blue flowers. Replant annually in cooler places. Delicate, romantic, with long stems.
Coreopsis hybrida or *C. lanceolata*	'Mayfield Giants' and 'Sunray'	Reasonably drought-tolerant plant producing a profusion of large daisy-like flowers. Lovely in meadow bouquets. Seven-day vase life.

RIGHT Echinops.

BELOW LEFT 'White Swan' echinacea.

BELOW RIGHT Aster.

Foliage

forage • scented • perennial • foliage • herbs • summer

cold tolerant • heat tolerant • long vase life • texture

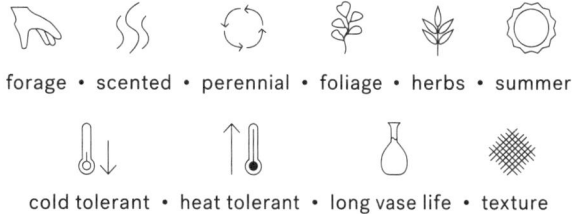

Secret to Summer Foliage

1 Foliage doesn't need to be green.

Flower-heavy arrangements with minimal foliage have been trending at weddings and remain popular. This is a challenge for florists trying to create impactful displays without blowing the budget. These white, silver and grey foliage varieties work beautifully in bouquets where green is not required:

- Dusty miller (*Jacobaea maritima*). A perennial in warm places, but re-sow in cold climates and it will be ready to cut just 4 months later.

- White sage (*Salvia apiana*). Highly valued as a ceremonial plant in many cultures, this drought-tolerant, aromatic plant likes well-drained soil. Only cut into green growth (not woody old growth) in order for new stems to be produced the following year.

- Sweet Annie (*Artemisia annua* and *Artemisia ludoviciana*) are hardy and evergreen in many climates. A cultivar called 'Powis Castle' has particularly long, strong stems but all cultivars will produce longer, straighter stems the more they are cut.

- Licorice plant (*Helichrysum petiolare*) is also known as trailing dusty miller and is a great option where a silver vine is needed.

- Lamb's ears (*Stachys byzantina*) for leaves that are irresistible to the touch.

2 Be adventurous with foliage in summer.

Summer is the best time of year to experiment with foliage. In winter, the choice is broadly restricted to evergreen trees and shrubs with most other plants dormant. In spring, the rising sap and new fleshy growth can risk stems flopping in an instant. Summer offers some innovative choices:

- Honeywort (*Cerinthe major*) has incredible pink-purple-blue flower heads atop milky blue-green foliage. So many colours on one stem. Unassuming on the plant but incredible in a bouquet.

- Beebalm (*Monarda didyma* and *Monarda fistulosa*). Smells of Earl Grey tea and has beautiful whorls of flowers on rich green stems.

- Mignonette (*Reseda odorata*). Lovely lantern-shaped seed pods and a great way to add texture.

LEFT Mighty eucalyptus trees surround the Flower Farm.

3 **Filler flowers bring foliage.**

Some plants grown for flowers also have useful foliage. High-summer favourites include:

- Cosmos
- Abelia
- Queen Anne's lace
- Zinnia
- Amaranthus
- Yarrow

4 **Beware the ravages of hot dry weather.**

A long, hot summer can be hard on plants, shrubs and trees. This makes hunting for foliage challenging, with many leaves looking a little worse for wear. Heat, wind, birds and bugs all take a toll in summer, so select leaves carefully. If you are planning for an important event, have a Plan B in case the leaves in your garden are looking a little tired.

RIGHT Cosmos is grown for its flowers but lovely, too, for the delicate, lacy foliage.

Airy Elements and Texture

Sweet Peas

summer • scented • easy to grow • fast growing • CCA

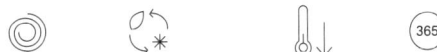

airy • succession sow • cold tolerant • annual

Plant summary

Buy me	Plant me	I flower	Cut me
Widely available as seed. Top five sweet pea cultivars for scent: • 'Matucana' • 'High Scent' • 'Shell Pink' • 'Mrs Collier' • 'Enigma'	Sow seed undercover into deep pots (this plant has long roots). Heat is required to germinate (a warm windowsill or a heat mat is perfect.) Then move pots to a cooler but bright spot. Plant outside when the weather warms in spring.	In spring and summer but is day-length sensitive (see p. 120).	Pick when there are still two unopened flowers at the top of the stem (these won't open but the stem may last longer). For a fuller look but shorter vase life, pick once all the flowers are open. Harvest first thing in the morning or late afternoon. Refresh the vase water every day.

Sweet, Sweet Secrets

1 **The secret to growing beautiful sweet peas.**

Often unavailable in florists, sweet peas (*Lathyrus odoratus*) are best when you grow your own. They are the Goldilocks of fragrance, neither too faint nor too overbearing, perfect for gently perfuming a room.

It's sometimes recommended to soak seed prior to planting. However, recent grower advice indicates this is not necessary, especially if the seed is fresh.

Sweet peas are incredibly cold-hardy, and many professional growers say the plants seem to grow better if they've suffered over winter. The secret is to sow the seed early enough in autumn so plants can establish and harden off outdoors (still in their pots) before the really cold weather arrives. The cold helps pinch out the stems, providing a robust bushy plant to put into the ground in spring (sow in late winter to early spring in very cold climates).

There's no need to pinch out if you grow your seedlings hard; side shoots will appear naturally. But if seedlings become leggy, nip out the top two leaves when there are four or more true leaves, to encourage bushy growth.

A note of caution. Mice love sweet pea seeds, even after the plant has germinated, and are indefatigable in their pursuit of this treat. Gardeners often overwinter seedlings in a mouse-proof cold frame or unheated greenhouse. Big commercial growers place their pots on a raised bench or plank of wood in unheated greenhouses. These benches have large overhangs preventing the mice from climbing up and over.

2 Sweet peas and day-length.

On the warm-climate Flower Farm, sweet peas flower for most of the year. We grow different varieties that flower at various times, and this timing is dictated by day-length.

Plants can detect the difference between day and night and some, like sweet peas, change their growing behaviour accordingly. Understanding this can unlock one of the least understood secrets to successful flower growing (see p. 123 for more detail).

Winters on the Flower Farm are short, with only 6 weeks where days have less than 10 hours of daylight. Three different types of annual sweet peas are sown: Spring, Winter and Summer Flowering. They are differentiated by the number of hours of daylight required to trigger bud formation and flowering:

- Winter types need a minimum 10 hours of daylight.

- Spring types need at least 11 hours.

- Summer types need 12 hours or more.

These specific types are planted at different points of the year for an almost continuous display of flowers.

Type	When to sow	Flowering time	Recommended varieties
Winter*	Winter	Autumn	Solstice Series: Crimson, Lavender
Winter	Autumn	Winter	Solstice Series: Rose, Pink and White
Spring	Autumn	Spring	'Mahogany', 'Triple G', 'Enigma'
Summer	Winter	Summer	'Dorothy Eckford', 'Turquoise Lagoon', 'Enchanté'
Perennial or Everlasting Pea	Any Time	Summer	'White Pearl' (Lathyrus latifolius)

*When sown in winter, the 'Winter' type sits around idly during summer (remember to keep up the water), but will commence flowering when the days shorten, and autumn arrives.

3 Perennial sweet peas for hot summers.

Sweet peas are also sensitive to heat and will run to seed when the weather becomes too hot. However, perennial sweet peas love the heat. These vigorous plants are drought-tolerant and can reach over 3 metres in height.

The plants need to be cut back (or ripped out) when they fall dormant, but otherwise are very low maintenance. The Latin name for the perennial form is *Lathyrus latifolius*; the annual sweet pea is *Lathyrus odoratus*. The *'odoratus'* suggests the difference between the two plants. While annual sweet peas are beautifully scented, the perennial flowering version sadly isn't.

THIS PAGE Sweet peas need support. We tie them to pyramids made from three stakes, secured at the top with string.

4 How to achieve long flower stems.

Traditionally, short flower stems (approximately 25 centimetres) are cut and used in small vases. For a more dramatic effect, cut entire sections of the vine with flower stems attached. This 'tangle' of sweet pea vines with flowers and seed pods is stunning in a vase. And the vine will recover quickly. Otherwise, for longer stems:

- Grow a Spencer series, known for its longer stems

- Plant at the correct time of year (if in doubt, late winter in cool places or autumn in warm places) so the plant can put on strong vegetative growth before flowering commences

- Tie the vines to a tall trellis

- Grow less-scented varieties; scent comes at the expense of stem length.

While some growers painstakingly snip off tendrils to achieve longer flower stems, breeder advice doesn't support this laborious activity. One less job to do!

5 Saving sweet pea seed is simple.

Of all the seeds to save, sweet peas are the simplest (large seeds, easy to collect) and most worthwhile, as sweet pea seeds are expensive. Sweet peas are self-pollinating, so won't cross-pollinate. Any seeds collected should remain true to type.

Collect the seed in a labelled paper bag once the pods are dry and papery. Store somewhere cool and dry. Take care with sweet peas as the seed, like the rest of the plant, is toxic.

Grow Me Instead

There are many vines useful in floristry. Sweet pea alternatives include:

- Love in a puff vine (*Cardiospermum halicacabum*). Cut when green lanterns have formed on the stem. Each lantern conceals black seeds. And each seed is daubed with a white heart as though painted on. Enchanting.

- Jasmine (*Jasmine officinale*)

- Cup and saucer vine (*Cobea scandens*)

- Clematis (*Clematis* x *durandii*, *Clematis integrifolia*)

- Hyacinth bean vine (*Lablab purpureus*)

- Nasturtium (*Tropaeolum majus*).

ABOVE Nasturtiums are lovely tumbling out of vases. Look out for unusual colours.

The Secret Influence of Day-length

While we are unable to control the weather and can feel overwhelmed at times by its unpredictability, we can use day-length to help us better understand our plants and their behaviour.

1 The predictability of day-length.

The longest day of the year is the summer solstice, approximately 22 December in the southern hemisphere and 20 June in the northern hemisphere. From this point, days gradually shorten until the winter solstice, the shortest day of the year (20 June in the southern hemisphere and 22 December in the northern hemisphere).

Unlike the weather, the annual pattern of day-length will not alter from year to year and is utterly predictable. Like the ocean tides and sunrise and sunsets, day-length information for your location and latitude is available in calendar format and can be counted on.

2 Plants can detect day-length.

It's well known that plants can detect the difference between day and night. But did you know they are also able to detect day-length and are even able to determine whether the days are becoming longer or shorter? When the day is 11 hours long, the plant will know if summer is approaching (lengthening days) or if winter is on its way (shortening days).

It makes sense that plants have evolved to know how much time they have to flower and reproduce. This kind of internal circadian clock dictates whether plants should put their energy into leafy growth or into flowers.

Fun fact: *The term day-length was coined because it was originally thought plants detected daylight. However, scientists later discovered that plants are in fact detecting the hours of darkness. While the common terminology of day-length remains in use, horticulturalists use the term photoperiodism.*

3 Growing better summer and autumn flowers.

Understanding the influence of day-length has allowed us to grow better flowers on the Flower Farm. Looking back, many of our past summer and autumn crop failures can be attributed to getting the day-length requirements wrong and sowing seed too late in the year. This meant the plants didn't have enough 'short days' to put on vegetative growth before the signal was given to the plants that 12 hours day-length had been reached and it was time to flower. This resulted in flowers on short stems, making for poor cut flowers.

Plants are roughly grouped as follows:

Long-Day Plants	Flower once the days are more than 12 hours long (either side of the summer solstice).	Many summer flowering plants: rudbeckia, Californian poppy, snapdragon, carnation, African marigold, asters, echinacea and some sunflowers.
Short-Day Plants	Flower once the days are less than 12 to 13 hours long.	Many autumn flowering plants: dahlias, chrysanthemums, lablab.
Day-Neutral Plants	Don't respond to day-length.	Geranium, amaranthus and some sunflowers.

Within the long- and short-day groups, some plants must have the requisite day-length whereas for others it's a preference, resulting in better flowers.

Tip: *Don't expect flowers the moment the day-length requirement is met. The plant will have received the signal to initiate flowering but it will take some time for the buds to form and for the flower to grow.*

Plant Profile: Dahlias are a great short-day plant. As days begin to shorten following the summer solstice the plants will ramp up flowering – gently at first before pumping out more stems than you can cut when days are less than 12 hours long.

4 Remember day-length when planning.

We find day-length to be a great guide in years when we're struggling to work around the weather. While climate and soil temperature impact plant growth, understanding a plant's day-length requirements will help you know when flowering should start.

We categorise our plants by their day-length requirements and note down the number of days to maturity (the period between seed sowing and harvesting). Normally the advised sowing date takes into account the day-length requirements of the variety.

In the event of a cold, late spring, sow your summer and autumn flowering seed under cover and wait until the weather has warmed before planting out. By starting the growing process even when the weather is inclement, we avoid day-length related challenges later in the season.

Plant Profile: Rudbeckia 'Indian Summer' is a summer flower because it needs long days to initiate flowering. While it will continue to flower into autumn, the stems will be shorter, and the flowers will become smaller as the days shorten. The plant takes 90 to 105 days to mature, so sow seed in early spring to get as many weeks of flowers as possible.

5 **Day-neutral plants.**

Day-neutral plants aren't impacted by day-length but that doesn't necessarily mean they will grow whatever the weather. They may be more impacted by the temperature or the presence/absence of water to initiate germination, commence flowering or start to set seed.

Plant Profile: Sunflowers have day-neutral varieties as well as long-day forms. It's helpful to know the difference when succession sowing. On the Flower Farm we sow long-day sunflower varieties until mid-summer, then switch to day-neutral varieties to still achieve long stems even as the days begin to shorten.

6 **Relax when the days are less than 10 hours long.**

Many plants won't grow when there is less than 10 hours of daylight. But the moment the clock ticks over that mark get ready to commence weeding! While temperatures may be no warmer, the plants (and weeds) have noticed the longer days (or rather shorter nights) and will begin to grow.

7 **Greenhouse growing.**

Have you ever driven by a large commercial greenhouse at night and wondered why the lights are on? Is everyone working late (possibly) or is the grower running up a hefty electricity bill to grow plants that require a longer day-length? Called 'day-extension', this is one of the ways commercial greenhouse growers can produce plants outside the normal growing and flowering season for year-round supply. This is also helpful for growers in cool northern climates where there are fewer long days and supplementary artificial daylight makes it more viable to grow long-day plants.

Another greenhouse grower's trick is to expose plants to longer periods of light at critical points in the growth cycle. This allows them to achieve a better cut flower than would be naturally possible. For example, if China asters receive over 14 hours of daylight during the first 4 to 5 weeks of growth, they will flower faster and on longer stems. Conditions that couldn't be replicated in the garden.

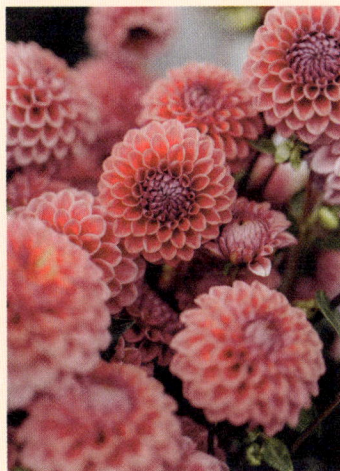

LEFT Early morning in the paddocks around the Flower Farm.

ABOVE As soon as the days start shortening, the dahlia abundance begins. This is 'Winkie Truffle', a Flower Farm favourite.

Day-length apps

Weather apps are incredibly useful. But make sure to also download a sunrise/sunset app. This will provide:

- Current day-length

- Day-length in an annual calendar format to help plan planting and predict flowering

- Sunrise and sunset times to assist with organising early morning harvests and evening jobs

- The elusive golden hour (half an hour with a magic 10 minutes or so) to capture those evocative flower photographs.

Make a note in your calendar of when the day-length for your location passes 10, 11 and 12 hours. Record any growth changes you notice.

Four seasons of flowers

Autumn.

The Secret to Golden Autumn Days

In many places, autumn arrives on quiet feet. The light softens, shadows lengthen, flower colours deepen and become more burnished. Garden and gardener take a beat and relax into cooler days and longer nights. If you listen carefully, you may even hear the plants breathe a sigh of relief.

Everyone's a little weary after the summer rush, ready to put their feet up. But not quite yet, because autumn is a time of incredible abundance in the cutting garden.

This is largely thanks to the generous and sunny dahlia. It may feel like this flower is everywhere, but the dahlia is rarely to be found at wholesale flower markets because the cut blooms travel so poorly.

Growing your own is the best solution and incredibly rewarding; the sheer volume of cut flowers from even a few plants, coupled with a flowering window as long as 5 months, feels positively decadent. And the tremendous variety of size, shape and colour will soon have you hooked. If you plan to sell cut flowers, this is the first plant you should grow. Local florists are likely to be keenly interested especially when sourcing flowers for weddings and events – and remember to plant lots of white.

As autumn eases towards winter and the dahlias fade, heirloom chrysanthemums are waiting in the wings. These lovely plants are indispensable in late autumn when large focal flowers are few and far between. Wonderful in Mother's Day bunches (in Australia and New Zealand) supported by heat-loving sunflowers, zinnias, celosia and amaranthus. Simply add a few ornamental grasses for movement to build beautiful autumn displays. This is the perfect time of year to mix fresh and dry elements, evocative of sun-baked fields awaiting autumn rain.

PREVIOUS PAGE Dahlias and amaranthus tumbling out of the windows and doors of an old stone cottage.

LEFT In Australia, watering holes hold out the last vestiges of green when all around is dry and parched. This precious life source was celebrated one warm autumn afternoon with sunflowers, quince branches and grapes tumbling from vines, ready to capture the golden, early evening light.

Hero Flower

Dahlias

CCA • long flowering • round • summer • focal

autumn • dried • trending • heat tolerant

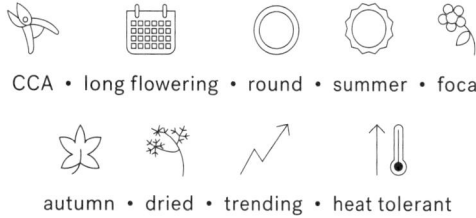

Plant summary

Buy me	Plant me	I flower	Cut me
As dormant tubers in winter and spring. Order early; the hunt for the best varieties of dahlia tubers has become competitive.	Plant tubers on their side, 5 to 10 cm deep with the eye close to a stake for support as the plant grows. Tubers are planted in spring after the last frost.	From early summer or mid-summer until the frosts arrive or late autumn in warm climates. Cut continuously to encourage repeat flowering.	Cut long and low into the plant. Sacrifice unopened buds for longer, thinner stems and more flowers as the season progresses.

Diva Dahlia Secrets

1 **Dahlias can be grown from cuttings, seed or tubers.**

Dahlias are generally grown from tubers, carbohydrate stores for next season's growth. The new plant grows from a swollen piece of tissue called the crown which is situated at the base of the old stem. Attached to the tuber via a neck, the crown contains 'eyes' that will emerge as shoots in spring.

Tubers vary in size and shape but generally look a bit like a chicken drumstick. Each tuber will have been divided from a much larger clump of multiple tubers. Once planted, this single tuber will multiply to form its own clump. This is why most growers dig and divide dahlia clumps every year. The investment of one single tuber can yield anywhere between three and ten new viable tubers.

If the tuber you've just received in the post doesn't resemble a chicken drumstick it may be a 'pot tuber'. Grown from a cutting in a small plant pot by a breeder, this dahlia will have formed a small, round clump of mini tubers. Once there are visible eyes, plant the entire clump in the ground with the old stem facing upright. The plant will flower as normal and form a large tuber clump by the end of the season. They're just as reliable so don't be concerned.

While most gardeners choose to grow from tubers it's often a good idea to take a cutting or two of a treasured variety. Or be adventurous and sow a tray of seeds to fill a separate seedling patch. Plants grown from seed may not make suitable cut flowers, but the bees will be happy as most of these 'lottery' flowers are likely to have open centres. There are pros and cons associated with each growing method.

LEFT A vertical curtain of chicken wire is suspended from hooks in the windows and doors of an old building. Dahlia stems are fed through holes in the wire to create a wall of colour. Perfect for a party installation. Positioning the flowers is akin to painting.

	Tuber	Cutting	Seed
Method	Most popular. Dahlias are commonly sold as dormant tubers.	Cuttings, once rooted in pots, can be planted in the ground. Many cuttings can be taken from a single tuber.	Dahlias are octoploids so rather than the normal two sets of chromosomes, they have eight. This results in great genetic diversity and a real seed lottery. Dahlias grown from seed are called 'seedlings' and each is unique.
Flower shape and colour	Same as parent, so appearance is predictable.	Same as parent, so appearance is predictable.	The flowers will be different to the parent plant and can vary widely.
Pros	Widely available, and the easiest growing method.	Fast and low-cost means of increasing plant numbers.	Save seeds from flowers you grow to breed your own varieties. Exciting to discover what might appear.
Cons	Dahlia tubers can be expensive and hard to find – particularly the sought-after varieties (so-called 'unicorns').	Potentially time consuming to maintain a humid environment while the cuttings form roots.	Low probability of growing a high-quality flower. But many fun 'mistakes' in the process.

ABOVE AND RIGHT The dahlia's incredibly diverse colour palette makes it autumn's most versatile flower.

2 Dahlias can be grown in pots, saving garden space.

Recent breeding has developed many varieties suitable for pots. Check with your local garden centre or dahlia grower.

We've found that the smaller collarette and pompon types are well suited to pots. As are some of the dinner plate varieties, which are shorter plants and less likely to topple over in a pot, despite their enormous flowers. Remember to stake well and if the plant is becoming top heavy, snip out the central stem to encourage lower, bushy growth. Dahlias grown in pots will require regular watering. Whether you live in a warm or cool climate, growing in pots has many advantages.

Warm climates: Dahlias hail from Mexico and love the heat. Provided the plants are watered regularly, you'll have an abundance of colour on an outside terrace or seating area through the longest, hottest summers and into autumn.

Cool climates: Plant tubers in pots undercover in a bright, frost-free place in the spring. Once the risk of frost has passed, harden off the plants and either place the pots outside or plant into the ground. This approach is especially helpful if you have a short growing season. They say that if you can grow tomatoes, you can grow dahlias.

ABOVE A bunch of Flower Farm 'seedlings' – dahlias we have grown from seed.

Growing dahlias from seed

If you happen to grow a 'seedling' so unique it may have potential, you'll need to first check that the plant is stable, healthy and stores well, a minimum three-year process. Dig the tubers of this new 'seedling' at the end of the season, divide and then replant the following year. Observe the plant and ask:

- Are the flowers the same colour, shape and form as last year?
- Did the tubers store well and is the plant productive?
- Are the stems long, strong and straight?
- Are the flowers held upright (i.e. not downward facing)?
- Does it produce lots of flowers?
- Are the flowers securely attached to the stem?
- Do the flowers have a good vase life?

Repeat the process for a third year. If the plant is still performing well, this dahlia is ready to be named and 'released' to growers. Some people share their 'seedling' tubers with other growers in different parts of the country in the third season to test how well they perform in varying climates.

3 **Water and dahlias**.

Dahlias are easy to grow once you understand how the plants' water needs vary across the growing phases.

Planting

- Plant a tuber with a fleshy eye or shoot into well-drained soil in spring after the risk of frost has passed. Hold off if the soil is waterlogged or sodden to avoid tuber rot. Conversely, bone-dry soil will desiccate growing shoots. If the soil is very dry, water before planting.

Shoots up to 10 centimetres tall

- Hold off watering at this stage. Until the tuber has formed roots, it can't absorb the moisture in the soil. Having said that, a light water is advisable if the soil becomes very dry or the weather very hot.

- If heavy rain is forecast, cover the ground with a tarp or even an upturned flowerpot (be careful not to damage any shoots) to prevent the soil from becoming too wet. If you regularly receive significant spring/ summer rain, grow dahlias in raised beds or pots to improve drainage.

Established plants

- Water in the evening regularly and more frequently in very hot, dry, windy weather. Monitor soil moisture levels. If the soil is bone dry or drying quickly, water the plants more often. If the soil feels very damp, reduce the watering.

- If a heatwave is forecast, water well in the lead-up to ensure the plants are fully hydrated. Leaves wilt in hot weather but bounce back in the cool of the evening.

- If a plant dramatically wilts, but its neighbours are fine, a rotten tuber may be the culprit. Wait a day or two, if it doesn't recover, dig up the tuber to investigate.

- Plants grown closely together under mulch will effectively shade the root zone and require less water in hot weather.

End of season

- As the foliage gradually yellows and the plant falls dormant, watering can cease. If significant autumn rains are forecast, dig up the tuber clumps and store somewhere dry.

- If your soil is very well drained dahlias can be left in the ground over winter in all but the coldest places. Cover the dormant plant with a thick layer of mulch for insulation. This saves time on digging and dividing.

Storage

- Dug tubers need a quick clean: wash off any dirt and lay somewhere with good airflow to dry or 'cure' the tuber skin. Tubers stored while still wet are more likely to rot (a constant risk for dahlia growers). For this reason, many gardeners divide the clumps before storage (eyes are also easier to spot at this stage). Store the divided tubers in boxes. One variety per box to prevent mix-ups.

- Store in a frost-free place under lightly dampened sawdust in a Styrofoam (or similar) box, with holes to assist airflow. Wooden boxes with the lid cracked make for a more attractive alternative. Check the tubers every few weeks – increase airflow and add dry sawdust if the tubers appear too wet, spritz with water if they're becoming wrinkly and dry.

Taking cuttings

- Plant a tuber in a pot filled with damp potting mix and place in a light and warm place.

- When the tuber has developed a 10-centimetre shoot, cut below a leaf node (making sure to leave at least one leaf node attached to the tuber).

- Trim the remaining leaves to reduce water loss.

- Plant the cutting in equal parts sand and potting mix. Place in a high-humidity environment (a mini greenhouse or overturned plastic box).

- Maintain the humidity and the cuttings will root in about 18 days.

- Grow on until the weather warms, harden off and then plant out.

ABOVE AND RIGHT Taking dahlia cuttings is a quick and easy way to increase plant numbers.

RIGHT **RIGHT** Dahlias are exceptionally prolific and with vigilant harvesting and deadheading will produce countless flowers. Float excess 'deadheads' in a bowl of water for a pretty table centrepiece. We used an old cattle trough to create this large ombre effect.

4 The secret to nudging sleepy dahlias into growth.

Every season, dahlia growers prepare to wake their tubers. Those with a fleshy eye or shoots are planted out once the risk of frost has passed because dormancy has broken, and the plant is actively growing. Other tubers are sleepier, with different varieties planted out over several weeks.

Waking dormant tubers:

- Once you've removed growing tubers, dampen the sawdust and move the box of remaining sleepy tubers to a brighter, warmer place.

- Check the tubers weekly and remove any that have developed eyes or shoots. Keep the sawdust damp. Truly stubborn tubers should be popped into a pot of damp potting mix.

- If a tuber fails to develop a shoot, it might not have a viable eye. These are called 'blind' tubers.

Some years, tubers are planted out until mid-summer. There will be fewer flowers on these late plants, but they will grow and store energy for the following year. These plants provide valuable late-season flowers and are often the first to waken the following year.

Experienced dahlia growers love smaller tubers. They are quicker to put out roots so can access water in the soil more readily than larger tubers that rely on carbohydrate reserves for longer. Something to remember when selecting your tubers. Bigger is not necessarily better.

5 **Dig and divide dahlias.**

Lifting dahlia clumps at the end of the season is like digging for treasure. How big will the clumps have grown? How many precious tubers will be available for the following year? It's a labour-intensive but fun aspect of dahlia growing.

Choosing when to dig depends on the climate. In cold climates, wait for frost to knock back the foliage and then dig the clumps before the ground freezes. In warmer climates, cut back still-green foliage to speed up dormancy. If rain is forecast, temporarily cover the cut, hollow mainstems with a bag or foil to prevent rainwater dribbling down into the stalk and rotting tubers. When digging, be careful not to knock tubers off the clump.

- Slice vertically with a spade in a circle of about 40 centimetres diameter around the old plant to sever the long fibrous roots.

- With two spades placed in the ground on opposite sides of the circle, push the handles apart. The spade blades will come together under the clump and lift it out of the ground.

- Gently wash off excess dirt. Take care not to rub at the dirt on the crowns of tubers as you may accidently remove precious eyes.

When dividing your dahlias, remember that tuber clumps grow in different shapes and sizes, so each clump is tackled differently:

- Begin by identifying the eyes at the top of the clump near the base of the old plant stem.

- Plan your first cuts so the best healthy tubers remain attached to the eyes you've identified.

- Make a score before cutting.

Eyes often occur in rings so once you've identified one, it may be possible to find others close by. After the easiest-to-spot tubers with eyes have been removed, it's often best to split the clump into sections before beginning again. Sometimes the eyes that are deeper in the clump are hard to locate and there are fewer available. It's fine to store small clumps over winter before dividing in spring when shoots appear.

Other dividing secrets:

- You will lose tubers along the way – have a compost bin ready and don't stress. It's part of the process.

- Invest in a simple magnifying light that clips onto the side of a table. This helps with spotting elusive eyes.

- Dip the cut end of a tuber in wood ash. This hastens sealing and drying.

- Lay tubers in trays for a few days to dry the cut ends before packing in sawdust for the winter.

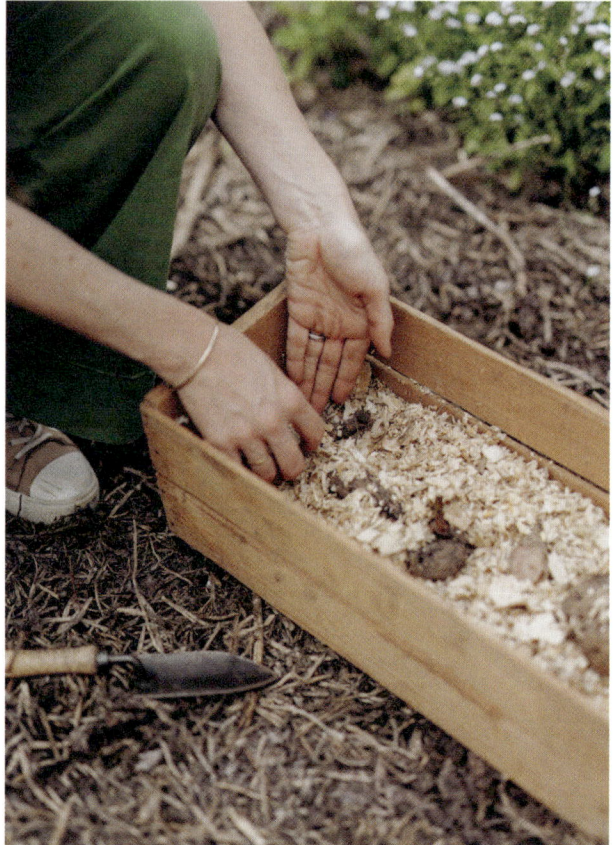

CLOCKWISE FROM TOP LEFT Digging
dahlia tubers in winter; isolating the
'eyes' that will grow next season;
divided tubers are stored in sawdust;
in spring dahlia tubers are planted
with the eye next to a stake.

6 **Harvest long and low for the best flowers.**

The secret to long stems is to cut above a pair of leaves, down deep into the plant. This usually means a stem with one flower and two or more sets of buds. Most people cut short stems hoping to spare those buds, but this is a false economy. Encourage the plant to branch low down so that, instead of a fat hollow stem like a broomstick, the plant will produce multiple strong, slim stems.

For longest vase life, harvest flowers that are three-quarters open in the cool of the day – if the petals feel papery, the flower is dehydrated or old. Remove any leaves below the waterline and immediately plunge the stem into a bucket of water to dislodge air bubbles. Let the flowers rest for an hour or two before arranging. Give the stems a further cut at a 45-degree angle before popping in the vase.

Decoding dahlia-speak

The best flower shapes for cutting are decorative, ball and pompon. While the dinner plate varieties are the reason many people get hooked on these incredible flowers, the short stems and massive flower heads make them harder to use in bunches.

Like tulips, dahlias are grown from living plant material, so they are rarely exported or imported due to the extensive and expensive biosecurity processes involved. With a few exceptions, this has resulted in every country (or region) developing their own special set of dahlias. There are similarities in the shapes (decorative, dinner plate, cactus, pompon) but the breeders' names and specific cultivars are different. Be mindful of this when swooning over photos from gardeners in different countries; they might not be available where you live.

Dahlia terms can be confusing:

- 'Decorative' is a shape category and not a description. This is the most popular shape for cut flowers and works well in bunches.

- There are multiple size variations which can be misleading. A 'small' dahlia measures a cool 120 millimetres to 160 millimetres across.

- A 'ball' is similar in shape but smaller than a 'decorative'.

- A 'pompon' is similar in shape again but smaller than a 'ball'.

- A 'ball' and a 'pompon' are almost totally round, like a lollipop on a stick.

RIGHT The Flower Farm's favourite dahlia, the smoky pink 'Winkie Truffle'.

Focal Flowers

Heirloom Chrysanthemums

autumn • trending • long vase life • round • heat tolerant

focal • easy to grow • low water • perennial

Plant summary

Buy me	Plant me	I flower	Cut me
Purchase rooted cuttings in spring (pre-order in autumn and winter). Ignore the varieties sold by big box garden centres or DIY stores as these plants are unlikely to be heirloom varieties.	Grow rooted cuttings in 8-litre pots or plant in the ground. Pinch back in late spring and take time to disbud in summer. Add slow-release fertiliser when you feed your rose bushes.	In the shorter days from mid-autumn. In many places this is just as the dahlias are finishing giving quality flowers, and just in time for Mother's Day (in Australia and New Zealand).	When the flower is almost fully open. The vase life is superb, lasting 2 weeks or more.

Heirloom Secrets

1 Choose heirloom chrysanthemums.

Most of us are familiar with the sturdy, softball-sized, 'disbud mums' and sprays of daisy-shaped chrysanthemum flowers. This small subset of the large chrysanthemum species is grown in a restricted range of colours and shapes. Commercial growers produce many hundreds of thousands of stems year-round in greenhouses in warm climates before air freighting them around the world.

However, in private gardens we can cultivate something rather more special. Heirloom varieties come in a wider variety of colours, shapes and sizes, with evocative names like brush and thistle, spoon, irregular incurve, pompon, quill, spider, anemone and reflex. They produce flowers from 2.5 centimetres to 20 centimetres in diameter, in a rich spread of colours including coral pink, metallic purple, bronze, burgundy, orange, red, apricot and yellow. These elegant flowers are much tougher than they look, being drought and heat tolerant, gracefully replacing dahlias as autumn progresses.

2 Take new cuttings every year.

While interest in heirloom mums is growing, this revival is still in its early stages and plants are not always easy to find. Heirlooms are generally sold as rooted cuttings and sent out in spring with pre-orders taken during autumn and winter. However, like the most sought-after dahlia tubers, demand outstrips supply. So be sure to subscribe to as many mailing lists as possible and get in *tout de suite* to order the best shades and shapes.

Although a perennial plant, heirloom chrysanthemums are more vigorous and less likely to succumb to disease when grown each year from cuttings.

LEFT The beautiful petal forms of a vase of heirloom chrysanthemums.

Once you have established your first plants, it's an easy matter to take cuttings and increase numbers each year.

Dig up chrysanthemum plants when they have finished flowering and developed vigorous new basal shoots. Snip off these shoots and plant into little pots to take root and establish under cover over winter. Be sure to label clearly.

Cuttings can also be taken from the stems. Remove the lower leaves and plant the cutting with just the top pair of leaves above the soil's surface. Place in a humid environment until roots appear. The old plant is composted, the new rooted cuttings planted out the following spring when the risk of frost has passed.

3 Learn the art of pinching out and disbudding.

Many chrysanthemums are big plants and can topple over in strong winds if not staked and tied as they grow over summer. 'Pinch out' the stem above a set of leaves for a bushier plant with a lower centre of gravity and more usable flower stems. Repeat this several times until mid-summer.

Pinching out will give more flower stems. Each stem will ultimately form many flower buds. To achieve large, impressive focal flowers you will need to 'edit' these buds. Left alone, each stem will produce a tightly packed spray of small flowers.

Removing some of the flower buds (in a process called 'disbudding') means the remaining will grow into larger flowers. We play around with disbudding, so we have some stems with sprays of small flowers, others with a few medium flowers and some with a single, very large flower.

Tip: *The 'pinched out' stems can be planted in pots as cuttings to take root.*

4 To pot or not?

At the start of the season, rather than planting rooted chrysanthemum cuttings in the ground, many experienced growers replant these cuttings into bigger containers (around 8 litres). Once the risk of frost has passed, these pots and plants are sunk into the ground. This ensures the chrysanthemum's roots – and willingness to spread – is contained and makes it easy to lift the plant and pot out of the ground at the end of the season to take cuttings.

Chrysanthemums are grouped into early and late flowering varieties. Although they are hardy, in places where early autumn frosts are common, the late flowering types will not perform well unless given some protection against the cold. If grown in pots these late flowering types can be lifted out of the ground and moved to a frost-free place away from the wind, perhaps a covered veranda or terrace.

For growers in warm climates where autumn weather is not too stormy and damaging to large flower heads, chrysanthemums can be grown directly in the ground. You will need to watch for runners and provide sturdy support, but watering will be easier and less time-consuming.

Tip: *If you grow chrysanthemums in pots sunk into the ground, keep an eye on watering, especially through the warm summer months.*

RIGHT A wide range of flower shapes and colours make heirloom chrysanthemums a great autumn cut flower to explore.

Grow Me Instead

If growing heirloom chrysanthemums proves too labour intensive, or you miss out on the rooted cutting sales, try these late-season beauties instead:

- Sunflowers in harvest colours (plant the seed in mid- to late-summer for flowers from mid-autumn onwards). The best sunflowers for this time of year are day-neutral varieties (see p. 123) as these will continue flowering even as the days shorten.

- Hydrangea flowers left uncut over summer will have antiqued by now and look divine when arranged en masse in a vase.

- Sedum 'Autumn Joy' or the improved 'Autumn Fire' are beautiful long-stemmed succulents with broccoli-shaped heads flowering from summer to late autumn. These sedums make surprisingly good cut flowers.

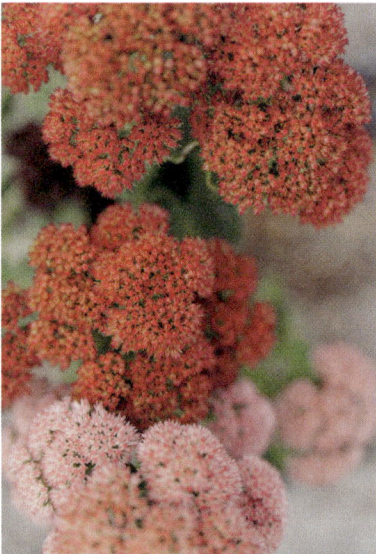

ABOVE Autumn flowering sedum.

RIGHT Green antiqued hydrangea in mounds on a log, flanked by vases of Jerusalem artichoke flowers and fiery Zinderella series zinnias.

Ikebana
The Japanese art of flower arranging

Ikebana means 'living flowers' or 'giving life to flowers'. In these carefully considered and symbolic arrangements, asymmetry and the use of negative or empty space are key. Students of this art spend many years learning to achieve a sense of harmony between flowers, container and setting. Ikebana has evolved over the centuries to arrive at many distinct styles, including:

*   *Heika* which includes *rikka* (standing flowers)

*   *Shoka* (living flowers)

*   *Seika* (flung flowers)

*   *Moribana* (piled-up flowers).

In Western floral arrangements, we tend to add multiple layers of foliage and flowers; in ikebana the emphasis is on adding as few stems and leaves as possible to compose an elegant shape and highlight the natural beauty of the flowers.

In recent years, there's been a trend in mainstream floristry for 'naked stems', where individual flowers are stripped of their foliage and placed higher than others in the arrangement. These ikebana-inspired arrangements benefit from a flower frog or kenzan that sits in the base of a vase or bowl to hold stems in place.

Filler Flowers

Celosia

easy to grow • low water • autumn • dried • heat tolerant

filler • texture • CCA • plume • trending • long vase life

Plant summary

Buy me	Plant me	I flower	Cut me
Easy to grow from seed. Find the best varieties online. Celosia plants sold in big garden centres are likely to be short-stemmed bedding types.	Sow seed under cover in early spring.	From mid-summer until late autumn (or the arrival of the first frosts).	When the flower is mature and the neck below the flower head firm, not floppy.

Secrets of a Sun Lover

1 **Celosia adores the heat.**

If you garden in a place with warm summers, you'll adore the tough, cheery celosia. Bright neon disco colours, cool shapes and fluffy textural elements make this a must-have plant. And if you live in a cooler part of the world, you can still grow this fun flower in a greenhouse or bright, protected space. Wherever you live, start seed under cover in very early spring as this is a long, slow grower.

LEFT Textural, fluffy plume celosias, in jewel and neon tones, are the ultimate heat lover.

RIGHT Fan shaped celosia and self sown calendula make a happy sight.

2 Cockscombs and plumes: curious celosia shapes.

There are three main species of celosia:

Flower Shapes	Recommended Varieties
Plume (*Celosia plumosa*)	Sunday series
Wheat (*Celosia spicata*)	'Flamingo Feather', Celway series
Cockscomb – Coral (*Celosia cristata*)	'Spring Green', Chief series
Cockscomb – Fan (*Celosia cristata*)	Neo and Bombay series

Some celosia varieties are 'branching' (multiple stems) and others are 'single stem', producing one flower.

	Branching	Single Stem
Varieties	All Plume and Wheat shapes. Some Cockscomb shapes.	Some Cockscomb shapes.
Pinch out?	Yes, at 20 to 30 cm tall. Remove the growing tip, leaving three or four leaves on the plant.	No
How many stems?	Prolific in season.	One
Spacing?	30 cm between plants.	Very tight, 10 cm x 10 cm. Close planting encourages longer stems.

3 Celosia and day-length.

Day-length-sensitive celosia needs between 90 and 120 days to mature, depending on the variety. The plant grows long stems during summer before flowering in the shorter, early autumn days. If planted too late, the plant will flower on short stems.

4 When to cut.

Cut celosias well before the flowers set seed. Seeds continue to mature even when the stem has been cut; late harvesting will result in a mess of glossy black seeds as you try to arrange flowers.

This is a bonus if you want to save seed (pop the flower head in a paper bag) but gives the flower a dirty look in the vase, particularly on the fan shapes. Celosia 'Pampas Plume' is a major culprit.

Grow Me Instead

Amaranthus

Amaranthus comes in a range of colours from red and coral to bronze, burgundy and lime green. Amazing when tumbling out of big vessels or hanging from suspended ceiling arrangements. It's a heat lover with similar growth requirements to celosia but allow extra space in the garden bed for these big, textural plants. The two forms most useful for cutting are:

- *Amaranthus cruentus*, with arched or upright plumes
- *Amaranthus caudatus*, much loved for its trailing rope-like tassels.

ABOVE LEFT *Amaranthus cruentus.*

ABOVE RIGHT *Amaranthus caudatus.*

RIGHT Draping long tassels in rich colours, amaranthus (or love-lies-bleeding) is a fantastic cut flower and looks best when the stems' large leaves have been picked out. Wonderful spilling out of oversized vase arrangements or in dramatic suspended installations at events. Hang bunches side-by-side to make a backdrop or sew fishing line through individual stem ends to make a striking table curtain.

Zinnias

If you have short summers and early autumn frosts, celosia's long growth period makes it impossible to grow to maturity. Fast growing, cut-and-come-again zinnias are a brilliant alternative.

Recent breeding has elevated this plant enormously, from gawdy, primary-coloured flowers to a more refined palette. Dreamy dusty pinks, salmon and peach tones, honey shades and greens make for a sophisticated choice.

There's also a range of flower sizes from the large 'Benary's Giant' and Queeny series to the diminutive Lilliput series and unusual frilly scabiosa-type zinnias like Zinderella.

For high-performance zinnias:

- Zinnias love warm weather. Sow the large seed directly into the ground once the soil has warmed, and in 75–90 days you will be cutting stems.

- If you experience late frosts, start zinnias indoors and plant out after the risk of frost has passed.

- Space about 20 centimetres apart and plant in full sun.

- Pinch out the central growing tip for a bushier plant with longer, thinner stems and more flowers.

- In warmer climates, succession-sow a second and third crop to provide a constant stream of zinnias during the warm summer and autumn months. They are susceptible to mildew, but if you have another crop coming along, you'll find it less traumatic to rip out affected plants.

- Choose colours appropriate to the season. Bright summer pinks and whites, then warm autumn salmon, honey and orange tones.

- Zinnias need support. Use horizontal mesh or staking.

- Regularly harvest or deadhead to prevent plants running to seed.

- Zinnias are true heat lovers, so do not store cut flowers in a cooler or fridge.

ABOVE Large flowered zinnia 'Benary's Giant Coral'.

RIGHT Scabiosa-type zinnia flowers from the Zinderella series.

Foliage

forage • easy to grow • low water • cold tolerant • scented

autumn • perennial • foliage • heat tolerant • texture

Scented Foliage Secrets

1 **Pick scented foliage for autumn bunches.**

In autumn, when dahlias are often the star turn, seek out scented foliage including herbs to complement these beautiful but generally unscented flowers. Fragrance is always available even as the weather cools, and at this time of the year the herb garden can provide rich pickings. Add perfume and whimsy to a bouquet with:

- Scented geranium

- Mint

- Pineapple sage

- Lemon verbena

- Lavender (with or without the flowers)

- Basil

- Nepeta (catmint or catnip)

- Agastache

- Myrtle

- Monarda (lemon balm)

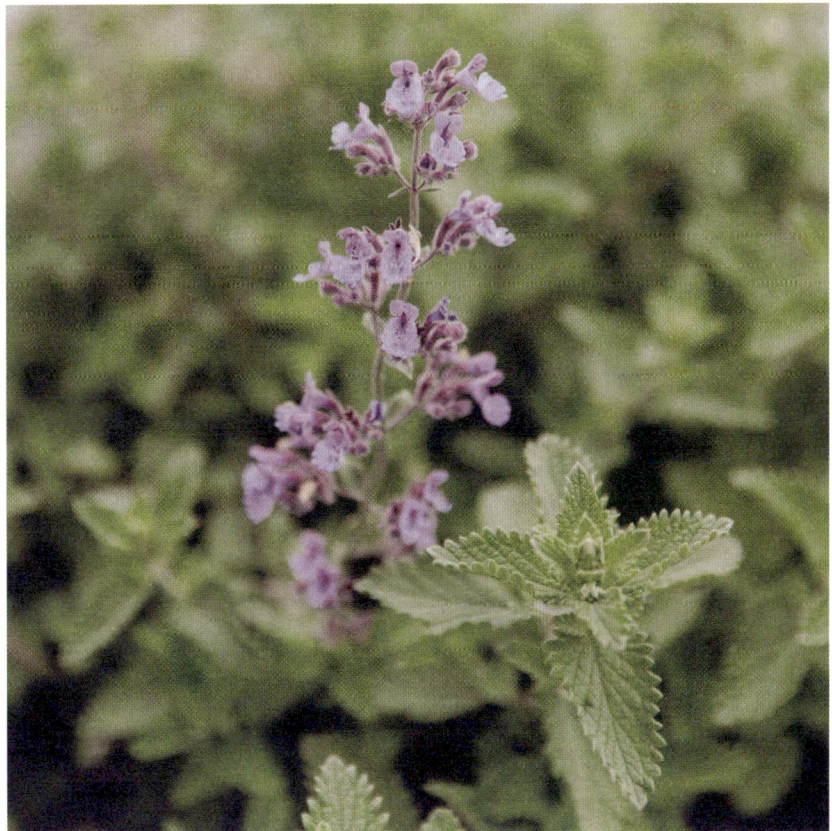

LEFT Glory vine glows in the autumn sun.

RIGHT Nepeta 'Walker's Blue'.

2   Colour match foliage to flowers.

Consider the earthy, warm tones of autumn flowers when foraging or cutting shrubs and plants. Ninebark (*Physocarpus*), cotoneaster, cordyline, purple hop bush (*Dodonaea viscosa purpurea*) and nandina all provide richly coloured foliage that works well in arrangements.

Another option is to forage from deciduous trees and plants as the leaves begin to turn. Oak, beech, birch and oakleaf hydrangea all suit arrangements as the leaves remain on the branches quite well. If the stem is very woody be sure to carefully slice up the stem to encourage water take up.

Have fun hunting for buds, hips and berries in autumn and winter to add rich jewel tones and texture to the vase. Rose hips, chillies, tomatillos or Cape gooseberry are wonderful. Look for the long tassels of the silk tassel bush (*Garrya elliptica*) or the bright berries of *Skimmia japonica* and holly (*Ilex*). Fruiting apple or pear branches make a dramatic seasonal statement.

3   Understanding eucalyptus.

Much loved in arrangements for its freshly scented, milky-blue round leaves, eucalyptus is an Australian native and florists' staple. When growing trees for cutting, it's important to understand only the immature leaves remain round; adult leaves on most trees become long and slender, losing their milky-blue colour. The exception to this rule is the small silver-leaved mountain gum (*Eucalyptus pulverulenta* 'Baby Blue'), which has silvery-blue round leaves into maturity and is grown commercially for the floristry industry. Those living in a cold climate where eucalypts are unlikely to survive the winter can grow the plant as an annual. Sow the dust-like seed under cover 10 to 12 weeks before the last frost date.

In warmer climates, coppice eucalyptus trees annually for a manageable size and to encourage new growth. Most eucalypts have a swollen ring called a lignotuber at the base of the trunk. A survival mechanism in the case of bushfire or animal damage, the lignotuber contains many dormant buds that will shoot into action after the trunk is coppiced.

Grow Me Instead

Commercially grown eucalyptus is frequently sprayed with pesticides to prevent defoliation from caterpillars. The damage can be significant, rendering stems useless for floristry. On the Flower Farm we don't spray, instead cutting eucalyptus during the summer and early autumn, snipping out the immature tips. Later in the season, by the time the caterpillars begin to make their presence felt, we opt for the milky-blue leaves of the Mount Morgan wattle (*Acacia podalyriifolia*).

TOP Blue gum eucalyptus.

BOTTOM LEFT *Acacia podalyriifolia*.

BOTTOM RIGHT Quince. Delicious to eat and beautiful tumbling out the front of a vase.

Airy Elements and Texture

forage • annual • low water • perennial • autumn • plume • airy • summer

Secrets of Texture and Light

1 **Dependable gypsophila.**

Baby's breath. A terrible name for a great plant that is indispensable in filling out arrangements or as a neutral backdrop. Flowers are airy and light but also incredibly strong and tough. A classic florist's go-to for a reason. Fresh or dried, these flowers are lovely in wild-themed bunches.

The plant comes in two forms, the annual (*Gypsophila elegans*) and perennial (*Gypsophila paniculata*). The perennial form is grown on the Flower Farm because the plant is drought and frost hardy, loves the very well drained soil and in warmer climates will flower throughout summer and autumn. Preferable to the annual form for cutting, the plants are bigger with taller stems and a longer flowering window but can be difficult to source.

Alternatively, succession sow some annual gypsophila – the 'Covent Garden' variety is readily available as seed. As a smaller plant it is a good option for pots and a better choice if perennial gypsophila is not winter hardy where you live.

2 **Ornamental grasses and dancing greens.**

Ornamental grasses with fluffy seed heads are lovely in autumn arrangements. Pampas grass is incredibly popular but a restricted weed in many places, so check your region first. Great grasses for cutting:

- Silver grass (*Miscanthus*), as much for its striped and banded leaves as the seed heads.

- Pennisetum also has colourful leaves and seed heads. Good cut flower varieties include 'Rubrum' and 'Fireworks'.

- Bear grass (*Xerophyllum tenax*) is used by florists to bind stems in bouquets.

- Briza (*Quaking grass*) and sea oats (*Chasmanthium*) are delightful when arranged to dance above a bouquet.

- While not a grass, Persian cress (*Lepidium sativum*) is an easy-to-grow annual. Let the edible cress go to seed for lush green seed heads.

3 **Cuttable crops.**

Agricultural crops including wheat, corn, barley and oats look incredible in flower arrangements. Pick green for a fresh accent or wait until the plants dry for wonderful biscuit hues. These grasses can easily be found in rural areas along roadsides (ask before attacking a farmer's crop) and are increasingly available as bouquet ingredients. For more chunky additions, seek out sorghum, millet and sweetcorn – glass gem corn in jewel tones is incredible.

LEFT Gypsophila clouds make a simple but beguiling party installation. Here, balls of chicken wire are filled with gypsophila stems and suspended from an old ladder. Eucalyptus adds a milky-blue contrast, and festoon lights bring drama. The 'clouds' can be left in place to dry.

Four seasons of flowers

Winter.

The Secret to Winter Beauty

Winter on the Flower Farm is a busy time. The mammoth task of digging and dividing dahlias, labelling and packing the tubers in boxes of sawdust lasts throughout the season.

It is wet, muddy work and after a long day on the farm it's lovely to have flowers in the house. We all spend far more time indoors over winter, so it's especially important to have a vase of something beautiful on the kitchen table to remind us that a garden never truly sleeps.

You might expect winter pickings to be slim but on the Flower Farm there's plenty of choice. Ornamental kale, stocks, wallflowers and other members of the Brassicaceae family are flowering. Where winters are milder, the hardy snapdragon is flowering (spring and summer flowering in colder places). And in both warm and cold climates the gorgeous perennial winter rose (*Helleborus*) flourishes. In more temperate climates, showstopping Australian and South African native flowers are at their best.

In cold climates, where snow lies thick on the ground and gardens are tucked up in bed, take the opportunity to grab a pair of secateurs, don a coat and head outside to forage for evergreen branches. Raid that box of dried flowers that you squirreled away during the warmer months to make a wreath or fill decorative bowls with pinecones and citrus. In the northern hemisphere, force hippeastrum (still commonly known as amaryllis) bulbs for festive colour or plant diminutive spring bulbs in terracotta pots for an early display.

Winter is the perfect time to fashion an indoor mini garden. Experiment with pot-et-fleur arrangements, where house plants are combined with cut flowers. Use shop-bought flowers if there's nothing in the garden to add to indoor plants and ferns. Choose an attractive vessel to fashion your arrangement – baskets, old timber boxes or ceramic bowls work well. And hunt out pretty containers to hold the cut flowers. It's a brilliant winter pastime.

PREVIOUS PAGE Early morning foraging for wattle.

LEFT This pot-et-fleur was made in late spring with sprigs of Canterbury bells, ornithogalum and roses to highlight the white spots on the begonia leaves.

ABOVE Harvesting hellebores.

Hero Flower

Ornamental Kale

long flowering • easy to grow • fast growing • winter

focal • cold tolerant • annual • round • long vase life

Plant summary

Buy me	Plant me	I flower	Cut me
As seeds. Double-check the packet to make sure it's an ornamental variety with bright colours and fringed leaves.	Sow seeds under cover about 2 to 3 months before the first autumn frost. Place outside once the seedling has several sets of leaves, harden off, then plant into the ground.	Throughout winter. Colours will be more vibrant once the weather cools.	At the base of the plant for the longest stem (smaller side branches may be produced but kale is generally treated as a single-cut plant). Strip off the lower leaves to leave a clean stem and tight, round 'flower' head.

Secret Beauty

1 Cabbages for the vase.

This little-known winter gem embodies many of the pleasures of growing your own cut flowers and has an ornamental beauty to rival many traditional cut stems. The decorative *Brassica oleracea* has a three-week vase life, is available throughout the depths of winter and is easy to grow from seed. Prepare to be surprised and delighted by how brilliantly it works in a bunch or a bouquet.

2 Plant closely for better stems.

Like other members of the Brassicaceae family, ornamental kale can grow to a monstrous size. Space seedlings no more than 15 centimetres apart. The tighter spacing will produce smaller and more usable flower heads. As the plants grow, carefully strip off the lower leaves; this will encourage the stem to grow taller and for a good round 'flower' head to form.

3 Freshen vase water regularly.

Ornamental kale has a long vase life, but it's important to regularly change the water to avoid an unpleasant cabbage odour. At the same time scrub the vase and re-cut the stem end on a 45-degree angle to encourage water uptake.

4 Protect from autumn insects.

If the early autumn weather is warm and the white cabbage moth or similar butterflies are still active, cover the young plants with a fine mesh. Caterpillar damage can be extensive. The mesh can be removed as the weather cools and the butterflies disappear.

LEFT Ornamental kale is a winter staple on the Flower Farm, delightful in bunches and bouquets.

Grow Me Instead

If ornamental kale isn't for you (but do try it once, you may be surprised), in temperate climates many Australian and South African natives, including banksia and protea, flower throughout the winter months. See Natives (p. 176).

RIGHT Stocks are great cool weather flowers. Apricot, light pink and lemon are most popular on the Flower Farm.

Focal Flowers

Stocks

easy to grow • cold tolerant • winter • spring • scented

focal • line/spike • succession sow • annual • fast growing

Plant summary

Buy me	Plant me	I flower	Cut me
As seeds. Check flower height first.	Sow under cover and plant out once seedlings have several sets of leaves. In cool climates, sow in late winter for spring flowers or in summer for autumn flowers. In warmer climates sow in autumn for early winter flowers then succession sow every few weeks for multiple harvests.	In cool temperatures. If the weather is too warm, flowers won't form. Flowers can be cut from this fast-growing plant in as little as 10 to 12 weeks after sowing.	Harvest when the bottom third to half of the stem's flowers are open. Flowers last a week in the vase and have a beautiful clove-like fragrance.

Stock Secrets

1 Stock is the best of winter's fragrant flowers.

There is something evocative, almost Proustian, about the old-fashioned, clove-like fragrance of stocks. In cool weather when the cutting garden is at its emptiest and fragrance is in short supply, this lovely member of the Brassicaceae family will grow and flower happily. The scent is perfect when brought indoors, a wonderful complement to log fires and hearty winter meals. Colours roam the spectrum from white and pink to blue, purple and apricot.

2 Select double or single flowers or grow the lot.

A packet of stock seeds provides a combination of single and double flowers. Recent breeding generally delivers a half and half mix. If you are determined to grow only doubles, you can select for these by examining the leaf colour of the cotyledons, the embryonic round leaves that first emerge from the soil. After chilling the seedlings at cotyledon stage to 4 to 7 degrees Celsius for 2 to 3 days, dark leaves indicate single flowers; lighter leaves indicate doubles. Most flower farmers plant the lot, using the doubles as focal flowers and the singles as smaller fillers.

Grow Me Instead

Hippeastrum
(Known as Amaryllis)

The stunning South African amaryllis is associated with Christmas in both the northern and southern hemispheres. In the colder north, bulbs are forced into growth by bringing them indoors to the warmth, providing a splash of colour while outside skies are grey. In the south, it's summer and the flowers are naturally in season. Amaryllis make wonderful cut flowers wherever you live, but last longer and look more Christmassy as a bulb planted in a rustic terracotta urn or festive container.

Growing amaryllis for Christmas

Flowers appear 8 to 10 weeks from planting, depending on the variety. Count back from Christmas and plant up bulbs over a succession of weeks, following these steps, to achieve a month-long display.

- Before planting, rehydrate the desiccated roots by soaking overnight in water.

- Select a tight-fitting pot. Just 2 centimetres of soil between the bulb and the side of the pot is perfect. For an eye-catching display, place several bulbs in a large pot, snug but not touching.

- The shoulder or top third of the bulb should sit above the surface of the soil. This part of the bulb is vulnerable to rot so be careful to water around rather than over the bulb.

- Keep the soil moist until the first shoot appears, then water more frequently, around twice a week while the plant is growing. Use tepid water. As the stems grow, they'll need support. Find some lichen-covered twigs to add even more charm to the display.

- Flowers will last several weeks, and very large bulbs will each produce several stems.

Amaryllis bulbs are expensive but if treated well will reflower year after year. These guidelines help ensure that the hefty bulbs soon pay for themselves:

- Give the bulb a liquid fertiliser twice a month when in flower.

- After flowering is over, plant the bulb in the garden where it can access the nutrients in the soil. Water during dry periods and continue to feed for a further 6 weeks.

- Leave the bulb in the ground until the foliage dies back in early winter. At this stage dig it up, cut off any remaining foliage and let the bulb cure.

- Amaryllis need a cool period before reflowering, so pop the bulb in the fridge for 10 weeks before planting if you don't get heavy frosts or want to grow them inside.

RIGHT AND BELOW Amaryllis provide a large focal flower against the pink, white and red tones of watsonia, kangaroo paw, dahlias and statice. For a northern hemisphere Christmas table, achieve a similar effect with paperwhites in pots, holly berries, poinsettias and hellebores.

FOLLOWING PAGE Wallflowers are another scented member of the Brassicaceae family and make great late winter to early summer filler flowers (climate dependent).

Filler Flowers

Biennials

easy to grow • cold tolerant • winter • spring

scented • filler • dried • umbel

Plant summary

Buy me	Plant me	I flower	Cut me
As seeds, widely available from garden centres or online.	Sow the seed under cover in summer and plant out once the summer annual beds are cleared in readiness for autumn. Keep up the irrigation until the autumn rains arrive.	From late winter in warm climates. From mid-late spring to early summer in cool climates.	Do a vase test to make sure the stems are ready for cutting – fresh green growth has little lignin and stems can wilt when cut.

Forgotten Secrets

1 **Biennials to the rescue.**

Old-fashioned cottage garden biennials, including sweet William (*Dianthus barbatus*), honesty and wallflowers, have been forgotten by many, which is a great shame. These plants make ideal cut stems and are especially valuable as they flower at a time of the year when not much else is around. Sow seeds in late summer, grow seedlings in pots out of the direct summer sun and plant out in autumn. Summer is a busy time in the garden, and many of us have decamped on holiday, so the poor old biennial is often relegated to the too-hard basket. Put a reminder in your calendar. You'll be so glad you did.

2 **Wonderful umbels.**

Umbel (or flat-topped) shapes are indispensable in bunches, softening the effect of vertical 'line' flowers (snapdragons, delphiniums, stocks and larkspurs) and acting as a filler between stems, adding layers to the bunch in an extremely dainty way.

Daucus carota 'Dara' (or chocolate lace flower) is a Flower Farm favourite. Also known as an ornamental carrot, its lovely, umbel-shaped flowers come in white, soft pink and burgundy shades. Flowering from mid-winter until early summer in our warm climate, this workhorse is eventually replaced by false Queen Anne's lace (*Ammi majus* or *Ammi visnaga*), flowering through summer. From summer into autumn, raid the vegetable garden for parsley and fennel; both produce lovely umbel-shaped flowers.

3 **Cut sweet William's stems before he flowers.**

Sweet William (*Dianthus barbatus*) is easy to grow from seed and will happily self-seed. It flowers for many months in a long, cool spring and the cut flowers have an incredibly long vase life. If you don't fancy the shape or sometimes gaudy colour of the flowers, consider using the stems before the plants flower. Florists use a non-flowering variety called 'Green Tick'; you can use any variety of stem, if you harvest before the flowers open.

4 Honesty – don't cut it in flower.

Honesty (*Lunaria annua*), also known as the money plant, flowers in winter and spring, and while its flowers are pretty, the lustrous autumnal seed pods are the jackpot we're after. These coin-shaped pods dry from delicate green in summer to papery brown in autumn. Hang cut stems upside down. When completely dry, gently rub the sides of the seed pods with your fingers. The brown outer layers fall away as if by magic – a very satisfying process – revealing translucent silvery disks on bare stems. Perfect for dried displays or Christmas arrangements.

Grow Me Instead

Hellebore

Emerging from the snow in cold climates like dainty jewels, the incredibly beautiful winter rose is there to remind us spring is just around the corner. Not a rose at all, the hellebore is very tough and comes in a vast range of colours from white, pink and purple to burgundy, yellow and even black.

Old-fashioned hellebores are shy, rather secretive plants with drooping, downward-facing flowers. Difficult to enjoy unless you happen to be a mouse. Recent breeding, however, has developed upward-facing flower heads, much more convenient for gardeners and flower arrangers alike with double, ruffled and bicolours available. As flowers age, they become tougher and papery, like hydrangeas, and many turn apple green in colour.

Plant Summary

Buy me	Plant me	I flower	Cut me
As potted plants from garden centres or online.	In autumn or winter into moist soil. Part shade in cooler climates and full shade where summers are hot. Perfect nestled under deciduous trees or large shrubs.	From mid-winter to mid-spring depending on the variety and the level of winter cold.	Pick once the stamens have dropped and a seed pod is forming for longer vase life.

TOP LEFT AND RIGHT Fresh and dried honesty seed pods.

BOTTOM Once petals are papery, hellebores can be bound with paper-covered wire or twine onto a ring base to make a pretty wreath. Tightly pack the flowers as they will shrink as they dry. Spritz with water to keep the wreath fresh.

Foliage and Texture

forage • perennial • foliage • easy to grow

winter • cold tolerant • texture • scented

Evergreen Secrets

1 Go green in cold climates.

In cold climates where frosts, snow and bracing winds make it difficult to successfully grow flowers for cutting in winter, vases need not languish empty. Grab a basket and head outdoors to forage.

While other seasons demand drama and colour, in winter a vase of evergreen foliage will freshen a room and provide a wonderful connection to the outside world. Cedar, fir, juniper, spruce, cypress and arborvitae make long-lasting fragrant vase subjects. Carefully slice a slit up the woody stem end to aid the uptake of water and avoid placing the vase too close to a fire or heater.

2 Flower buds on trees can be 'forced' into opening.

In late winter (or early spring in cold climates), cut branches with swelling flower buds and bring inside to the warmth. Placed in a large glass vase, these stems make for a captivating display, as the flowers gradually open. The following respond well:

- Japanese quince (*Chaenomeles speciosa*). Beautiful coral, peach-white or pink flowers appear in the depths of winter on bare stems.

- Forsythia (*Forsythia suspensa* or *Forsythia × intermedia*). Bright yellow flowers are a foretaste of spring.

- Witch hazel (*Hamamelis*).

- Pussy willow (*Salix discolor* or *Salix caprea*). The furry grey buds of pussy willow are delightful. When they have burst, enjoy the vibrant new leaves as they unfurl. With regular water changes the stems are likely to develop roots and can be planted out.

- Fruit tree branches. A perfect use for 'sucker' stems that need removing from the tree.

3 Add unexpected texture.

An unexpected something can lift winter arrangements. Before pruning roses, cut a few stems with ruby red or deep orange rose hips. Or look for berries and fruits that have persisted into winter. Chillis grown in a greenhouse can be cut on the stem. Gently cupped in their papery husks, Chinese lantern and tomatillos are a delight in the vase.

4 Mix fresh and dried stems.

Dried flowers come into their own during the winter months and are a long-lasting solution to many a dark corner. Dried stems can also be threaded into vases of fresh foliage or flowers. Blowsy dried hydrangea, jewel-toned paper daisies and cheery yellow billy buttons work particularly well.

PREVIOUS PAGE Cutting the furry catkins of pussy willow.

ABOVE, LEFT AND RIGHT The cutting and kitchen gardens meet in this wild winter arrangement. Chillies, Cape gooseberry and rosehips catch the late afternoon light and provide pops of colour. Burnt orange paper daisies, kangaroo paw and cold-tolerant calendula further enrich the palette. Softer pastel tones come with apricot and lavender coloured stocks, tall pineapple lilies and purple isopogon flowers. A wild tangle of nasturtium completes the picture.

PART 3

Flowers

Native.

The Secret to Southern Hemisphere Stars

Imagine coming in from a chilly mid-winter garden. In your hand, a bunch of freshly picked flowers in rich shades of mustard, carmine, pink, vivid orange and yellow. Big flowers that last 2 to 3 weeks in the vase without dropping petals, and can be dried to add a bright, textural note for another 6 to 9 months. This 'unicorn' bunch will be familiar to many Australians and South Africans.

In floristry and gardening, plants endemic to Australia and South Africa are often grouped together and called natives as they generally thrive in similar conditions. Comprising woody trees and shrubs but also smaller bushes, soft-leaved plants and tiny blooms, the flowers' often coarse texture and warm tones evoke the landscapes of a hot, dry homeland.

While some natives are hardy to minus 7 degrees Celsius (and perhaps colder but this is poorly tested), it's their heat and drought resilience that make them desirable in a changing climate. These are the lowest maintenance plants grown on the Flower Farm – and a wonderful choice if you have little time to garden but still long to fill your home with bold, long-lasting colour.

With their robust tolerance for hot, dry conditions, and a striking beauty that suits contemporary interiors, South African and Australian native cut flowers are growing in popularity around the world. Along with the famous king protea and Geraldton wax, recent breeding is bringing new varieties. Fashionable florists are on the hunt for unusual flowers like the enchanting, slightly quirky, butter-yellow featherhead (*Phylica pubescens* 'Hydra') from South Africa.

Most excitingly, breeders are grafting varieties to combine plant characteristics. This new way of growing native flowers, where the best flower is grafted onto the toughest root stock, yields plants that thrive in a wider variety of conditions.

In the main, South African and Australian native plants require similar conditions for growing. The soil should be well drained, slightly acidic and with low phosphorous levels. While these plants don't love a rich soil, it is a misconception that they don't require fertiliser. They generally appreciate an annual feed with a speciality native blend that is low in phosphorous.

PREVIOUS PAGE AND LEFT Banksias and proteas bring warmth and rich colour to autumn and winter days.

Availability of native plants

Other than paper daisies and everlastings, which can be easily grown from seed, most native plants are best grown from tubestock or small potted plants. In Australia, New Zealand and South Africa these plants are readily sourced at good garden centres and specialist nurseries. If possible, select varieties endemic to your region. This will bring more pollinators and bird life into the garden and the plants will stand the best chance of growing successfully. Otherwise, select a plant to match your conditions and consider the space available. Some varieties will grow into very large shrubs or trees but can be managed with pruning.

Flowering Season	Focal	Filler	Foliage	Cones, Nuts and Seeds
Spring	*Banksia coccinea** Waratah Leucospermum	Paper daisies* Isopogon Boronia Wax flower Dryandra* *Philoteca pubescens* 'Hydra' Flannel flower*	*Aulax cancellata* Leucadendron 'Silver Tree' Leptospermum (tea tree)	Berzelia Leucadendron 'Sacred Cone'
Summer	Woolly banksia* Bird's nest banksia*	Billy buttons* Kangaroo paw* Rice flower Verticordia* Flowering gum	Eucalyptus* Acacia* Aulax cancellata	Brunia*
Autumn	*Protea repens* *Banksia menziesii* *	*Phylica pubescens* 'Hydra' Grevillea*	Leucadendron* Eucalyptus* Acacia*	Brunia*
Winter	*Protea neriifolia* King protea	Blushing bride Cootamundra wattle (Mimosa) Thryptomene Sea urchin hakea* Geraldton wax	Leucadendron* Myrtle*	Gumnuts

* Flowers over multiple seasons – peak indicated

CLOCKWISE FROM TOP LEFT
Protea 'Sylvia', Eucalyptus leaves,
Beaufortia sparsa, *Banksia speciosa*.

Hero Flower   Proteas

long flowering • easy to grow • low water • long vase life

focal • heat tolerant • perennial • dried • texture • trending

Plant summary

Buy me	Plant me	I flower	Cut me
As small potted plants from specialist nurseries.	In autumn for warm climates or spring for cool climates.	From autumn to spring with a peak in winter, depending on variety.	Once the flower has coloured, but before the centre of the flower is fully visible.

Secrets from the South

1 **There's more to proteas.**

The South African Proteaceae family is the most useful of woody cut flowers with a delicious spread of varieties and colours occurring at different times of the year. These species, all known as proteas, are especially lovely:

- *Protea neriifolia*. Stunning pink flowers with feathery black edges in autumn and winter.

- *Protea compacta*. Bountiful pink flowers over winter.

- King protea (*Protea cynaroides*). Enormous bowl-shaped flowers in greenish white, deep or soft pink in the warmer months.

- *Protea repens*. White and pink flowers in autumn.

Other, equally captivating members of the Proteaceae family have very different flower shapes and names:

- Blushing bride (*Serruria florida*). The most delightful, dainty winter flower in ivory to pale pink, custom designed for bridal bouquets.

- Leucadendron. Red, orange and yellow tones. Coloured bracts form at the end of long stems, making them brilliant for cutting. Flowers in summer, autumn and winter.

- Leucospermum. Also known as pincushions, the bright orange, yellow and red coloured flowers glow when massed atop small shrubs in spring to early summer.

LEFT Proteas respond well to pruning, which is necessary for keeping these large plants to a manageable size.

2 **Pruning proteas.**

Proteas flower on a two-year cycle. It's important only to prune stems that have flowered that year. Prune every stem and you will lose next season's crop. Cut relatively hard, leaving 10 to 15 centimetres of healthy stem with leaves. Don't deadhead immediately below the flower head as new growth will appear from this point leading to bigger, more unwieldy plants.

3 **Plant banksias to flower in summer.**

Most proteas flower in the cooler months. The banksia group offers many alternatives into summer with big, brush-like flowers in rich reds, oranges and yellows. The flowers work well with summer colour schemes. The unusual, deeply toothed foliage (rather like someone's taken to the plant with a pair of scissors) is also incredibly useful. Favourites for cutting:

- *Banksia coccinea*. Popular in floristry for its striking grey and scarlet, sometimes orange, flowers.

- *Banksia menziesii*. Known as firewood banksia with lovely orange/brown flowers.

- *Banksia prionotes*. The acorn banksia is especially arresting with large orange cylindrical flowers occurring at the end of branches. Easy cutting.

- *Banksia speciosa*. The so-called showy banksia has lovely, creamy yellow flowers set against silvery, deeply toothed leaves.

- *Banksia burdettii*. Similar flowers to the acorn banksia on a rounded, bushy shrub.

- *Banksia attenuata*. Tall, yellow, candlestick-like flowers.

- *Banksia baxteri*. A lovely creamy yellow with rounded, rather than cylindrical, flower shape giving it the common name of bird's nest banksia.

4 **Creating a winter bunch without large flowers.**

If proteas and banksias won't happily grow where you live, either source the stems from your local flower market, or get creative in building a more inventive focal point in an arrangement. When florists are unable to source suitable large focal flowers, they often deploy a clustering effect.

- Mass a group of smaller flowers together to create the focal point (a bunch of blushing bride, paper daisies or dried ranunculus).

- Substitute with other large, dried flowers such as dahlias or wide umbel-shaped flowers including bronze fennel flowers.

- Use dried allium heads. The 'Purple Rain' variety is larger than a grapefruit.

- Glue cones, nuts or pods onto wooden stakes to form a false stem and design a textural focal point.

RIGHT AND BELOW A lovely cooling statement in white, green and yellow using *Banksia Prionotes*, *Banksia Speciosa*, *Banksia Burdettii*, *Protea Repens*, blue gum (*Eucalyptus globulus*), and winged paper daisies (*Ammobium alatum*).

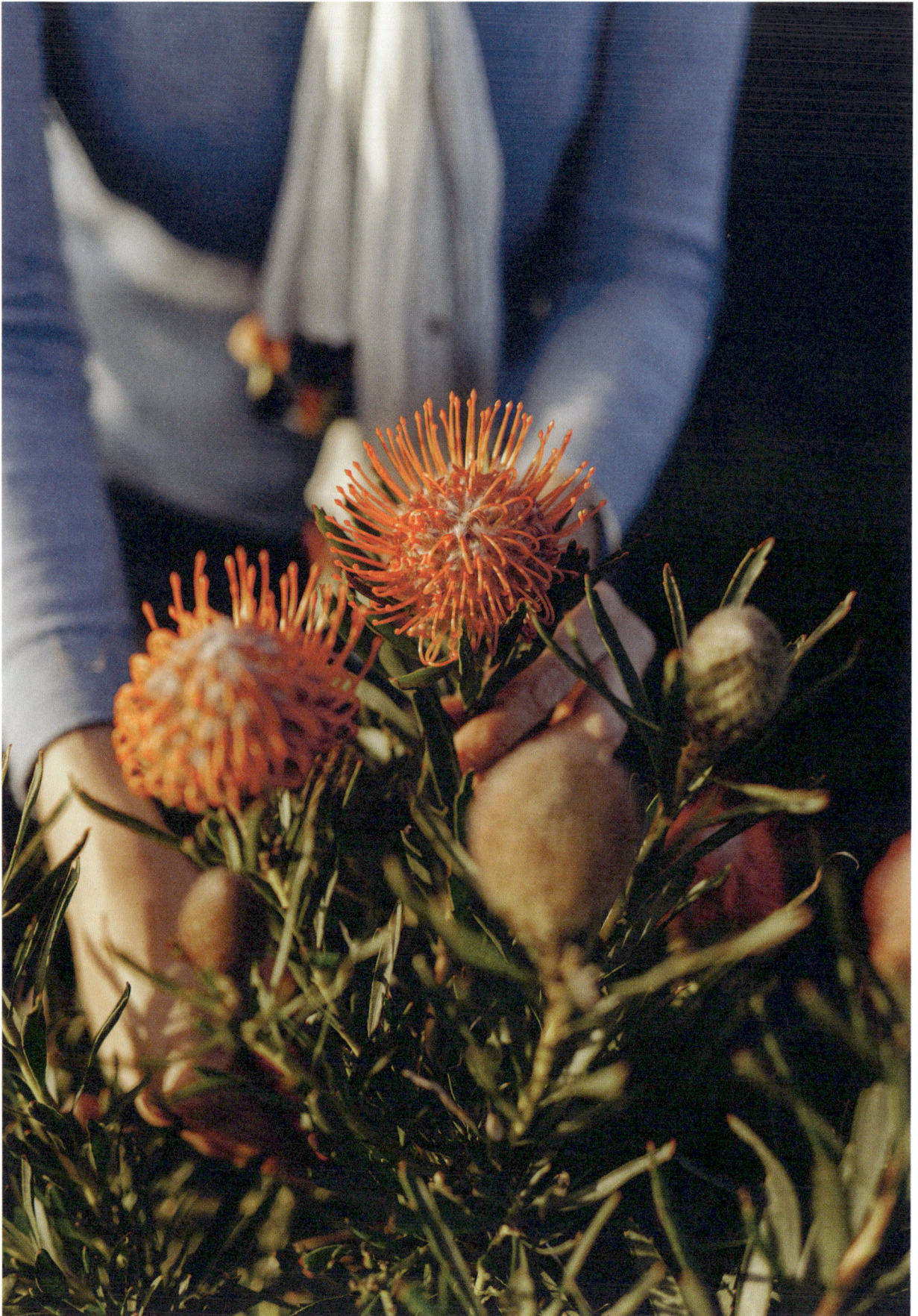

Focal Flowers

Leucospermum (Pins)

easy to grow • low water • spring • long flowering • heat tolerant

focal • perennial • globe • long vase life • trending • texture

Plant summary

Buy me	Plant me	I flower	Cut me
As plants from garden centres or specialty growers.	In autumn for warm climates or in spring for cool climates.	In late spring to early summer.	When the nylon-esque pins are still attached to the centre of the flower.

Pincushion Secrets

1 Handle with care.

The lesser-known leucospermum or pincushion flower makes a great cut stem but is underused by many florists, maybe because it doesn't travel well in bulk. The round flower heads have delicate-looking nylon-like pins. While the pins are tough, the flower heads are at risk of snapping off the stem. Handle with care when harvesting and moving in and out of buckets and vases.

Often two or more flower heads are produced on one stem. These sit closely and sometimes fuse together as they grow. This can be difficult to manage in an arrangement. Removing the second bud (disbudding) when the flowers are immature solves this problem.

2 Pins to the rescue.

Transport issues aside, this is a wonderful and striking cut flower that looks brilliant massed in the vase. It's worth finding a well-drained spot in your garden if you live in USDA zones 9–11 (or equivalent). Flowering prolifically for 2 months, pins are helpful in filling a gap in late spring when proteas are finishing but before banksias are in full swing. Coming in rich yellows, reds and oranges, with recent breeding throwing out some compelling coral hues, these exotic flowers do look very much like pincushions, although some more closely resemble sea urchins!

Grow a range of different cultivars and hybrids to extend your flowering window:

- *Leucospermum glabrum* 'Dancer'. Pale red and orange flowers on long stems.
- *Leucospermum* 'Rigoletto'. Deep orange-red flowers in late spring.
- *Leucospermum* 'Veldfire'. Yellow with splash of red.
- *Leucospermum* 'Titan'. Orange-red flowers.
- *Leucospermum* 'Tiara'. Pale orange/yellow flowers.

LEFT Make a statement with the dramatic pincushion flower.

Grow Me Instead

Isopogon formosus

Flowering from late winter into spring, the evocatively named rose coneflower, a member of the Proteaceae family, pairs well with winter brassicas and spring bulbs in a mixed bunch. The almost woody fruiting cones linger on the plant long after the flower has faded, adding an interesting textural element to displays. Cut stems are most attractive when the mauve-pink flowers and earthy brown cones are both present. The shrub is a great choice for coastal gardens in USDA zones 8 and 9 (or equivalent) with dry summers and wet winters.

ABOVE AND RIGHT The pretty isopogon, or rose coneflower.

Blushing Bride

A member of the Proteaceae family, blushing bride (*Serruria florida*) is perhaps the most romantic native flower grown on the farm and incredibly popular for weddings. Delicate petals in ivory or soft pink are borne on slender stems with needle-like foliage. It flowers winter through spring and grows very happily in a pot. The cut flowers have malleable stems, are light and last well out of water, making them perfect for flower crowns, button holes and corsages. Bind small bunches onto a headband or a piece of soft wire with string or paper-covered wire.

ABOVE Ivy, the Flower Farm flat-coated retriever, proudly models the blushing bride flower crown, accessorised here as a dog collar.

Filler Flowers

Paper Daisies / Strawflowers

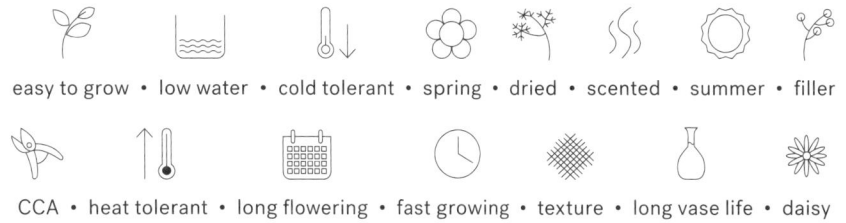

easy to grow • low water • cold tolerant • spring • dried • scented • summer • filler

CCA • heat tolerant • long flowering • fast growing • texture • long vase life • daisy

Plant summary

Buy me	Plant me	I flower	Cut me
Easily found as seed. Check the Latin names (see below).	Hardy over winter in warm climates, allowing spring and autumn planting (spring only in cool climates). Sow under cover 6 to 8 weeks before planting out.	About 80 days after germinating.	Make the first cut 'long and low' to encourage branching. Harvest before the centre is visible as the flowers continue to open in the vase.

Solving Daisy Secrets

1 **Know your (botanical) names.**

In horticulture every plant has a botanical name, but gardeners often prefer to use common names which can vary around the world. The case is even more muddled with paper daisies as there are multiple common names and multiple botanical names. It's important to check the standardised, unique plant name when ordering paper daisy seeds to be sure you are buying the correct plant.

Many paper daisies, also known commonly as strawflowers or everlastings, are native to Australia. Available in a wide assortment of colours and hues, these pretty flowers are lovely as fresh stems in a vase but even better as a dried flower. Indeed, the delicate, papery petals feel almost pre-dried. Better still, the colours don't fade as the flower dries. Paper daisies prefer a sunny spot with good drainage.

Common Name	Latin Name	Notes
Paper daisy or (bracted) strawflower	*Xerochrysum bracteatum*	The most popular variety for drying. This Australian native comes in a wide range of colours from gold, burgundy and red to soft pink, white and peach.
Paper daisy | Helipterum	*Rhodanthe chlorocephala*	An Australian native with black flower centres and white or pink papery petals.
Paper daisy | Immortelle	*Xeranthemum annuum*	Native to eastern Europe and western Asia. Fine stems with a pastel meadow-flower vibe.
Winged paper daisy	*Ammobium alatum*	Another Australian lovely with small white helichrysum-shaped flowers on long statice-shaped stems.

2 **Saving paper daisy seed.**

Keep cutting your paper daisies for a longer flowering window and lots of stems. After that, it's simple to collect seeds by breaking off the flower heads and securing in a paper bag. The seeds will slowly 'explode' away from the central seed head. Sow into seed trays and plant out when big enough to handle or direct sow into the ground in autumn (germination rates will be lower).

Grow Me Instead

Kangaroo Paw (*Anigozanthos*)

Exactly what is says on the tin. A brilliant cut flower in sunset hues that bears a striking resemblance to a kangaroo paw; even the texture is furry. Breeding has developed smaller plants in lovely pastel colours of blue, pink, violet and turquoise. Some of these newer varieties are fussier than their taller cousins and better grown in containers.

Most plants are tall, around 2 metres high, with richly coloured flowers in red, lime green, mustard or orange. Incredibly profuse, they are a star turn on the Flower Farm. Harvest the long stems just above a bud to get a second cut from every stem. All kangaroo paw flowers dry beautifully, retaining their textural tone.

Billy Buttons (*Pycnosorus globosa*)

Everyone's favourite Australian native flower. Billy buttons' bright yellow spheres emerge on long straight stems from a mound of soft silvery foliage. The more regularly flowers are cut, the longer the plant will continue to send up flowers. Billy buttons are even more useful as dried flowers, retaining their cheery yellow colour for months. The perfect flower to have on standby for winter dried bunches or for lean times when there's a gap in your garden's flowering window. Prefers a well-drained soil.

Gomphrena

Neither Australian nor South African, this plant is nevertheless a great alternative if you don't have space to grow the tall paper daisy. Gomphrena has shorter stems but is a vigorous plant, producing a profusion of papery red, white, pink and bicoloured flower heads that dry brilliantly. Harvest before the lower bracts start to peel away. Gomphrena 'Audray' is particularly good for cutting.

PREVIOUS PAGE Drying paper daisy flower heads.

CLOCKWISE FROM TOP LEFT
Beaufortia sparsa; kangaroo paw; billy buttons; banksia series Dryandra.

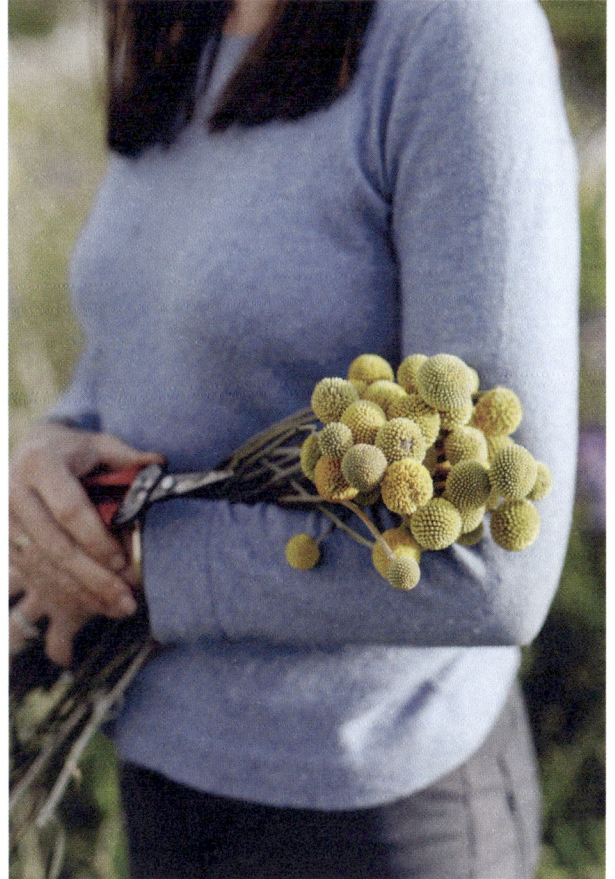

Growing Australian and South African Native Plants from Seed

The Australian and South African climates can be harsh, and the continents' native plants have evolved to thrive in often dry, low-nutrient soils, even adapting to fire. In fact, fire plays an important role in the germination of many Australian native plants. Extreme heat or the presence of smoke residue triggers germination, allowing seedlings to establish with less competition from the plants destroyed by fire.

This extreme measure of preventing germination until a precise set of conditions is met is known as a germination inhibitor. In this instance seeds have evolved to germinate only following the presence of heat or smoke.

While it's faster to grow natives from tubestock or small plants, these are not universally available so you might need to grow from seed, a fiddly process but very rewarding. Many Australian online seed sellers ship internationally. As always, check which species are permitted in your area.

SMOKE TREATMENT ESSENTIAL	IMPROVED GERMINATION	SMOKE TREATMENT NOT REQUIRED

• Boronia
 	
• Isopogon
 	
• Rice flower (*Pimelia*)
	• Feather flower (*Verticordia*)
	
	• Hakea
	
	• Protea family including:
	
	  ◦ *Protea cynaroides*
	  ◦ *Protea compacta*
	  ◦ Leucospermum
	  ◦ Leucadendron
		• Kangaroo paw
		
		• Scarlet banksia (*Banksia coccinea*)
		
		• Red flowering gum (*Corymbia ficifolia*)
		
		• Silver dollar gum (*Eucalyptus cinerea*)
		
		• Tea tree (*Leptospermum*)
		
		• Mulla mulla (*Ptilotus*)
		
		• Waratah

Websites retailing Australian or South African native seed will usually sell ready-made smoke-infused papers or smoke-treated vermiculite. However, you can make your own:

- Carefully and safely burn a handful of twigs and leaves from native Australian plants or trees.

- Collect the ashes and soak in water for 24 hours.

- Sieve out the ash remnants and soak your seeds in the smoke-infused water for 6 to 24 hours or until the seeds are swollen.

- Immediately sow the seeds into a seed starting mix.

TOP Spring flowering Australian and South African natives.

ABOVE Richly scented boronia.

RIGHT Tall kangaroo paw.

Foliage

Leucadendron

easy to grow • low water • perennial • foliage • long flowering

heat tolerant • line/spike • dried • long vase life • texture

Plant summary

Buy me	Plant me	I flower	Cut me
As plants from specialist growers (northern hemisphere) or regular garden centres (southern hemisphere).	In autumn for warm climates or spring for cool climates. Check the winter hardiness (tolerant to –5°C) and growing conditions are a match to your area.	Throughout the year depending on variety.	Depending on the type (see below).

Secret Foliage Alternatives

1 **Versatile leucadendron.**

Leucadendron are dioecious with separate male and female plants. The female plants produce bracts (resembling stiff petals) and later attractive 'cones' on the branch's tip, making for a great cut stem that lasts 3 weeks in the vase. While the female plants are most commonly recognised, the male plants produce eye-catching flowers with unusual colour combinations. These have the added advantage of attracting bees and other pollinators to your garden. For the longest vase life and best aesthetic, make sure you cut the male flowers soon after they have opened and preferably before they've been pollinated (black dots will appear on the flower once pollination has occurred).

When cutting stems from the female plant, ensure you don't cut too soon otherwise the stem tip will droop. We harvest at different stages depending on the variety:

- Some are grown for their bracts. 'Safari Sunset', for example, has long, attractive, burgundy-red bracts. It is the Flower Farm's favourite leucadendron for cutting.

- Others have incredible cones. 'Fantasy Sunrise' has lovely yellow bracts but really shines when the contrasting red cone appears in spring.

- 'Purple Haze' is a unique variety and is useful for cutting, both for the metallic purple foliage and the silvery cones.

LEFT *Leucadendron discolor* cultivar.

2 Flower, Filler or Foliage?

Although technically a flower, the versatile leucadendron is often used as foliage by florists in a bunch or arrangement. When a bunch needs more colour, texture, or visual interest but not necessarily more bulk, turn to the mild-mannered leucadendron. Many of the stems cut on the Flower Farm are 60 centimetres or longer and make excellent highlights at the back of a bunch. Dwarf varieties also exist, and these are perfect for growing in pots, a good solution if your soils are damp and heavy.

3 Pruning is key to long, strong stems.

If you plan to cut flowers the leucadendron plant, like most natives, will need to be well managed to produce long, strong stems. Pruning begins early in the life of the plant to ensure a good base shape.

Following the final harvest in spring, prune any remaining stems back to 10 to 15 centimetres (use your secateur handles for an easy measuring guide). This will ensure strong, vertical new stems are produced the following season. Otherwise, plants can become quite raffish, trailing across the ground.

Our favourite leucadendrons for cutting:

- 'Safari Sunset'
- 'Winter Gold'
- 'Highlight'
- 'Orientale'
- 'Inca Gold'
- 'Goldstrike'
- 'Jester'
- 'Summer Sun'
- 'Pisa'

Winter wreaths

While dried wreaths are great for year-round decoration, there's something special about a traditional evergreen winter wreath. Wherever you live, celebrate the winter solstice (the shortest day of the year) by hanging a fresh evergreen wreath on your door. They are so easy to make. Wire bases are readily available or make your own by creating a circle of soft branches and tying the ends together.

Use reel wire (wire on a reel) or jute string and bind small bunches of greenery to a base. Moving in an anticlockwise direction, ensure each bunch conceals the stems of the previous. When you have covered the whole base, tuck in flowers, pods and other decorations. The wire used to bind the foliage should be tight enough to hold the stems in place but use mossing pins if more support is needed. Mini wreaths can be used as napkin holders.

Grow Me Instead

If your growing conditions don't suit Australian and South African native plants (too cold, too wet), there are many European and American native shrubs perfect for cutting:

North America

- Willow. North American native varieties with beautifully coloured catkins include *Salix gracilistyla* and *Salix melanostachys*.

- Andromeda (*Pieris japonica*) is best cut in bud before the flowers have fully opened. It has beautiful white flower panicles although pink varieties can also be found.

- Winterberry (*Ilex verticillata*) has amazing berries in bright red, orange and gold tones depending on the variety. Wonderful for northern hemisphere Christmas displays.

Europe

- Viburnum. With varieties native to both Europe and the US, this is a great group of plants. Snowball viburnum (*Viburnum opulus*) and *Viburnum tinus* are two superstars in the vase.

- Willow (*Salix cinerea*). Widely found and a great candidate for 'forcing' in late winter to early spring.

- English holly (*Ilex aquifolium*). If you want red berries for Christmas displays, it's wise to cut stems and put them in a bucket of water in a cold shed or garage protected from the birds. Berries harvested this way will last 3 to 4 weeks.

- Ivy (*Hedera*) is lovely in winter wreaths and whenever you need anything long and tough but entirely malleable.

Airy Elements and Texture

Flowering Native Shrubs

easy to grow • low water • perennial • airy • texture

long flowering • heat tolerant • long vase life • scented

Plant summary

Buy me	Plant me	I flower	Cut me
As plants from specialist nurseries or grow from seed.	In autumn for warm climates or spring for cool climates.	Grow a range of varieties for season extension.	Wait a couple of years before cutting flowers and stems so plants can establish.
			Harvest before flowers are fully open, for the longest vase life.

Shrubby Secrets

1 **Tough but sweetly scented.**

Not all Australian and South African native trees and shrubs produce large flowers; many are festooned with dainty, sometimes scented blooms and foliage. The fine texture of these plants adds movement and lightness to a vase of big woody natives. The following fine-leaved native plants make the best cut flowers:

- Geraldton wax (*Chamelaucium uncinatum*) produces fragrant sprays of edible waxy white, pink and red flowers.

- Rice flower (*Ozothamnus diosmifolius*) is a delight; the flowers are like puffed rice and dry really well. Comes in white and soft pink.

- Feather flower (*Verticordia*) brings soft, plume-like flowers in a range of yellows, oranges and pinks.

- Flannel flower (*Actinotus helianthi*) is an Australian classic; the soft, cotton-white flowers add a delicate matt tone to a bridal bouquet. Grows well in a pot.

- Boronia (*Boronia heterophylla*) has a strong, sweet perfume; use sparingly in bunches.

- Eristemon (*Philotheca myoporoides*) flowers in the depths of winter and has delightfully scented foliage and star-shaped flowers.

- Thryptomene (*Thryptomene micrantha* or *Thryptomene stenophylla*) is also recommended. This woody shrub is drought-tolerant and flowers from winter into spring.

LEFT Wattle flowers are a late winter staple in Australia.

2 Pompoms galore.

Sea urchin hakea (*Hakea petiolaris*): a curious name and a curious plant but a firm Flower Farm favourite. In late autumn, globular clusters of flowers appear fixed directly to the woody branches. Though they do resemble sea urchins, pompom is an equally apt description. The flowers' colours gently morph from cream to pink to red. The perfect colour combination to dance above heirloom chrysanthemums and proteas in autumn vases.

The golden wattle (*Acacia*) is the floral emblem of Australia. It flowers across the country, throughout much of the year, peaking in early spring. Small, fluffy yellow flowers in spikes or trailing tassels (depending on the variety) add a pop of colour to mixed native bunches and bring a splash of sunshine to the late winter landscape. Cootamundra wattle is especially good as a cut flower with the ferny foliage throwing purple and blue tones. Wattle is also known as mimosa, particularly in the northern hemisphere.

Flowering gum (*Corymbia ficifolia*) trees produce weighty gumnuts like pendulous bells and make ornamental additions to wreaths; however, it's the sea of flowers covered in buzzing pollinators in late summer that's most beguiling. Big branches of fuzzy coral, red, pink and white flowers make for a showstopping display at their peak and look incredible in the vase.

3 Growing natives in pots.

If conditions are unsuitable for natives where you live, hunt around for smaller varieties that do well in containers. Some, like the lovely blushing bride (*Serruria florida*), seem to prefer growing in a pot. Consider pot growing if:

- Heavy frosts mean you need to place pot plants under cover in winter (just make sure there is sufficient light inside as most natives are evergreen)

- Soil is heavy clay or not well drained

- Soil is very alkaline (although proteas tolerate lightly alkaline soil)

- There is no full-sun, open position elsewhere in your garden

- The flower beds have been well composted over the years, making the soil too rich for most natives.

Remember to water regularly and feed with a specialist native fertiliser annually. Potting mix must be very well drained (natives hate wet feet). Add 10 per cent perlite and some coarse sand.

As most natives are sun lovers, place them in an open spot in your garden. It's visually quite effective to cluster pots together in a group. This also helps shade the base of the pots, keeping the roots cooler and reducing the amount of water needed. Recommended small natives for pots:

- Yellow bells (*Geleznowia verrucosa*)

- Boronia ('Carousel' or 'Lipstick')

- 'Little Prince' protea (*Protea cynaroides*). A compact king protea bred especially for containers.

- Blushing bride (*Serruria florida*)

- Banksia 'Birthday Candles'

- Yellow-trailing pincushion (*Leucospermum prostratum*)

CLOCKWISE FROM TOP LEFT
Geraldton wax, sea urchin hakea, *Philotheca myoporoides*, flowering gum.

Flowers

Dried.

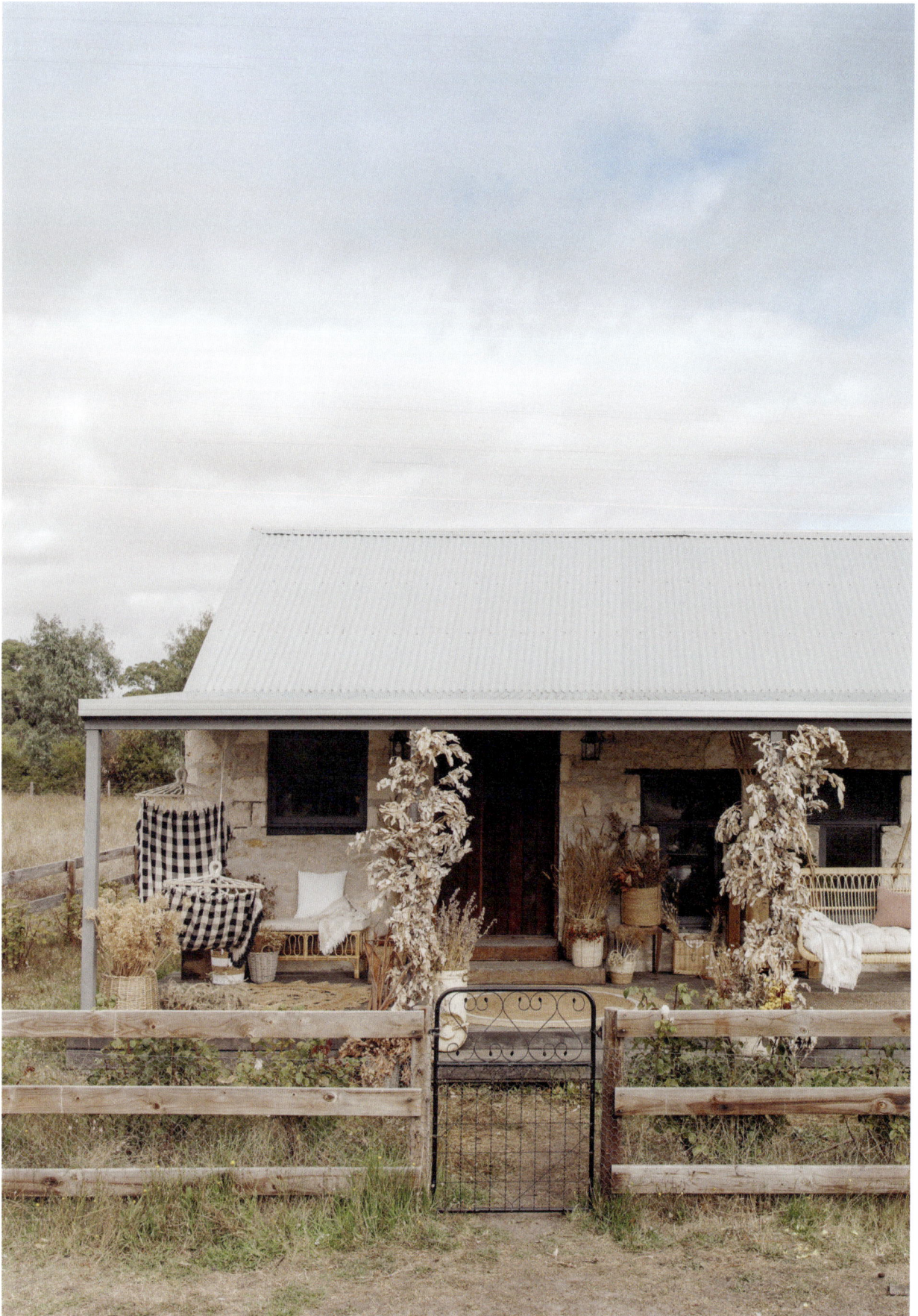

The Secret to Beautiful Dried Flowers

Some plants seem designed by nature for drying. Paper daisies spring to mind (the clue is in the name). But many unexpected plants, those with lush, delicate and transient flowers, also dry extremely well. Dahlias and roses in late summer and ornitholgalums and ranunculus in spring. Drying surplus blooms is a sustainable way of making use of every single flower, preserving the cut stems' ephemeral beauty.

If you would like to grow plants to preserve in this way, start with small flowers known to dry well like paper daisies, statice and billy buttons. And while you wait for these easy-to-grow flowers to mature, have a forage around the garden; there's always something to be found to bring indoors.

In the world of floristry, there's a growing appreciation of dried botanicals, a celebration of the whole plant, not just the delicate papery flowers. Dried grasses, arching branches, cones, gumnuts and skeletal flower heads all possess a special beauty. By using these once overlooked materials, it's possible to add texture and nuanced colour to arrangements and installations.

Stems can be gathered and dried at any time of the year. Even in the depths of winter, there is beauty in fallen branches and hard, woody pods and cones. And on the Flower Farm in spring, any tulips that remain uncut are left to run to seed. Some produce enormous seed pods, even with purple stripes. These are incredible picked green, and as they dry and open, a whole new aesthetic is revealed.

At the height of summer, when days are hot and rain less frequent, look to naturally occurring grasses, those untouched by lawnmowers, that have grown tall and set seed. Dried to a golden biscuit colour and dancing in the breeze these abundant grasses are a delightful addition to your hoard of cut stems. On the Flower Farm we harvest armfuls of naturally sown paddock grasses, tie the slender stems into small bunches and store (when completely dry) in boxes for future months. Lovely woven through fresh and dried arrangements.

By autumn, celosia, amaranthus, statice and gomphrena are ready for cutting, the rich jewel tones perfect in Persian-carpet style dried arrangements to warm and colour our homes during the colder months.

Whatever the season, the perfect space for drying should be dark and warm with good airflow. Avoid sunny rooms, as UV light fades colour. Sheds or garages work well but laundry rooms are typically too moist.

PREVIOUS PAGE An old high-roofed barn next to the Flower Farm has been set up with ropes and hanging mesh for drying flowers. The large open door is covered to block out light. Once dry, the flowers are stored flat in boxes.

LEFT AND ABOVE Blue gum branches dry in-situ on the flower studio terrace, decorated with dried grasses, jute rugs and rattan swing seats. Perfect for a lazy summer weekend.

Hero Flowers

long flowering · dried · round · focal · texture · CCA

Many focal flowers in fresh arrangements can be successfully dried, including garden roses, Italian ranunculus, dahlias, proteas and banksias. The large size of these flowers means the cut stems continue to create a focal point in an arrangement even when dried.

Dried essentials

Pick me	Dry me	Use me
Perfect flowers in their prime make the best dried stems.	Larger flowers take longer to dry. Ensure each flower is fully dry before storing to avoid mould.	Use as focal flowers to give a pop of colour. They look especially good at the base of an arrangement sitting over the vase lip or edge.

Secrets to Dry For

1 **Drying ranunculus and roses.**

The Italian ranunculus is a beautiful, generous cut-and-come-again fresh flower with a lush, juicy feel. The dried version is equally beguiling, although with a very different aesthetic: petals like tissue paper provide a faded, antiqued charm. With larger flower heads and multiple layers of petals, Italian ranunculus make better dried flowers than ordinary garden ranunculus.

When picking, it's important that the rose or ranunculus flower is no more than two-thirds open to ensure the petals remain attached to the flower base as the bloom dries. Fully open, mature flowers may fall apart while drying.

Colours alter as petals dehydrate and it's fun to play with different shades to see which you like best. Rich colours tend to deepen – a lush red rose becomes even more intense, the colour darker; blue tones become more prominent in hot pink flowers – candy pink ranunculus become a soft lavender pink when dried; pastels fade, and whites become sepia-hued.

Dried rose buds are gorgeous when the colour of the petals is visible, but the flower is not yet open. At the end of the season don't forget to dry hips for winding into wreaths and adding a colour burst to winter displays.

To dry flowers simply remove unwanted foliage and hang upside down to dry in small bunches out of the sun to protect delicate pigments.

LEFT Italian ranunculus, hanging in small bunches to dry.

2 **Drying dahlias.**

The secret to incredible dried dahlias is to:

- Hang each stem individually (i.e. not in bunches)

- Pick when the flower is two-thirds open

- Focus on yellow, orange, hot pink, red and sunset tones (white dahlia flowers tend to brown)

- Choose 'decorative', 'ball' and 'pompon' types.

On the Flower Farm, parallel strands of string are strung across a dedicated drying barn. Horizontal mesh or old drying racks are also useful. For large flowers, paper clips or elastic bands are used to hang each flower individually, ensuring it doesn't touch its neighbour. Overcrowding can result in misshapen flowers. When the flower is fully dried, store away from sunlight in between sheets of tissue paper in a cardboard box.

3 **Drying proteas and banksias.**

These heavy, woody flowers have tough stems, so flowers won't wilt when out of water. This means the stems can be dried upright in a vase and enjoyed throughout the drying process. If there are any leaves obscuring the flower bracts gently snip these off. As the flowers slowly dry, the colours change, becoming richer and more concentrated before gently fading over several months.

Once proteas have been dried for some time (6 months or more depending on humidity levels), the central parts of the flower tend to loosen and can be pulled away to reveal a beautiful timber-toned protea 'star' at the flower's base. At this stage we tend to repurpose the protea stars, using them as accents in an arrangement rather than as a focal flower.

King proteas (*Protea cynaroides*) are some of the most dramatic flowers in gardening. Metre-long stems and enormous, bowl-shaped pastel pink or greenish-white flowers make these a real scene stealer. The flowers have an extremely long shelf life, a month or more when fresh, remaining attractive for years after being dried. Brilliant in a large, heavy vase or as part of an oversized installation. Make sure those heavy stems are securely tied in place.

Australian and South African mixed native bunches dry very well. After enjoying the fresh flowers in a vase for a week or two, lift from the water, and trim the stem ends, remove the leaves and any part of the stems that sat below the water line, then hang the flowers upside down to dry. We call these 'fresh to dry' bunches.

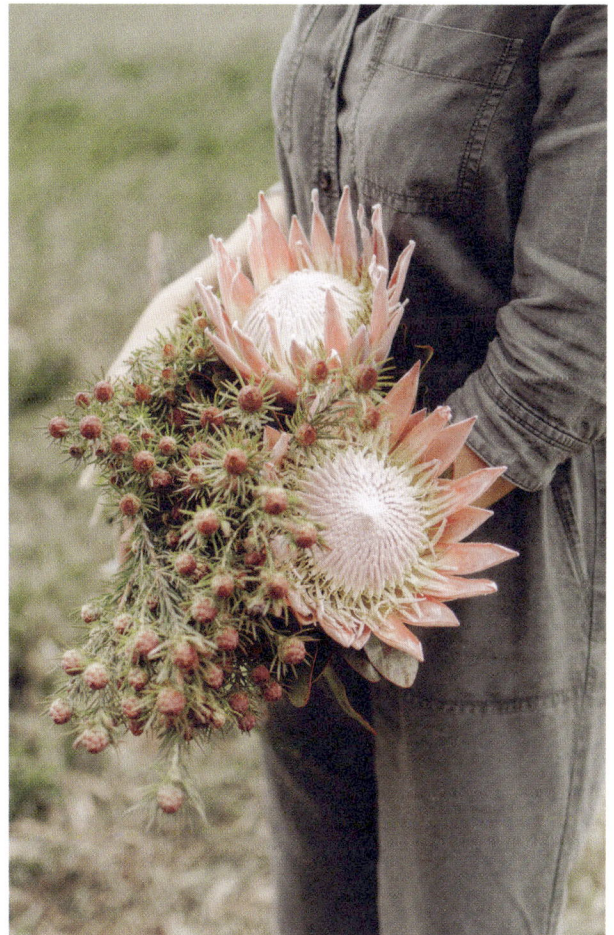

TOP Dahlias are suspended individually to dry.

RIGHT AND ABOVE King proteas, incredible fresh and when dried.

Focal Flowers

Hydrangeas

perennial • summer • autumn • focal • dried

globe • round • trending • texture • long flowering

Dried essentials

Pick me	Dry me	Use me
For drying, leave the flowers on the plant for between 6 and 8 weeks before harvesting.	Remove leaves and place the cut stems in a vase with just a few centimetres of water. As this water evaporates the flowers will slowly dry.	Mound in a fishbowl-shaped vase. Or sit just above the vase edge in a mixed arrangement. Brilliant in large installations.

Hydrangea Secrets

1 **Hydrangeas are one of the loveliest dried flowers.**

Hydrangeas make for a pretty and romantic dried flower, so useful when creating dramatic installations. Unlike most other flowers selected for drying, with stems cut in their prime, hydrangeas for drying are harvested towards the end of the growing season, allowing you to enjoy the flowers in the garden all summer long. Protect the plants from full sun during the warm months to prevent flower edges from browning. In warmer climates it's wise to grow hydrangeas in shade, such as beneath a deciduous tree.

By the time stems are cut, the flowers have begun to 'antique' or change colour in the most fetching way, the petals taking on a slightly papery feel. Place in a vase with a few centimetres of water. Don't change or top up the water. Allow the water to slowly evaporate and as it does the flowers will dry.

Dried flower heads are more muted than the clear pastels of the fresh flower, but this sepia tone is evocative and, somehow, even more lovely. The resulting stems are exceptionally valuable as large, focal flowers in dried arrangements.

Tip: *When cutting hydrangeas to use fresh or to dry, remember this useful hack for wilting flower heads. Submerge the whole stem, flower head and all, into a big tub of water. The petals will absorb water and 12 hours later, the flower should bounce back.*

LEFT Harvest hydrangeas towards the end of the growing season when the flowers have taken on a romantic 'antiqued' hue.

2 Elegant dried arrangements.

Hydrangeas are a go-to stem for dried arrangements. Begin with a ceramic or opaque vase or vessel, as dried stem ends can look messy behind glass. Pop the hydrangea stems in first, using the large flower heads to cover the lip and base. Other dried stems can then be threaded through, with the large hydrangea flower heads acting as an anchor, holding slender stems in place.

Fill a basket with dried hydrangea flowers (using a ball of chicken wire to hold the stems) to brighten a dark corner or decorate an unused fireplace over summer.

Tip: *Naturally dried flowers are a long-lasting way to preserve an ephemeral flower, but they don't last forever. Once petals are brown and gathering dust, onto the compost heap they go.*

Sun-bleached Stems

Preserved white flowers have become very popular. These stems are artificially coloured and bleached to avoid the brown or yellow staining that may occur when white flowers naturally dry in the sun. Sprayed with softeners and glues so the petals hold, these stems last for a very long time. However, the chemicals involved in this process are environmentally damaging.

Naturally sun-dried and sun-bleached flowers are a much more sustainable alternative, and perfectly aligned to the organic, softer look that is so popular. And it couldn't be easier. Simply hang cut stems and flowers in full sun, being sure to protect from the rain and wind. Drying times vary according to the thickness of the stem and density of the flower head. Be sure to check on colours as the stems dry.

Bring foliage with existing white, grey or blue tones out of the sun as soon as the stems are dry but before the light tones start to brown. Quick-drying stems such as gypsophila can either be brought inside the moment they're dry or remain in the sun for longer so rich biscuit hues develop. Stems that respond well to sun-drying:

- Blue gum eucalyptus
- Baby's breath (gypsophila)
- Basket flower
- White cornflowers
- White scabiosa
- Yarrow or achillea (light shades)

- Ranunculus (white and light shades)
- Allium seed heads (ornamental and leeks or onions that have gone to seed)
- Poppy pods
- Grasses such as pussy tails

- Artichokes
- Hydrangea flower heads (once already dried)
- Honesty
- Woolly banksia

Tip: *Delicate dried flowers can shatter when handled. Lay a damp cloth over the stems or place in the fridge for half an hour. The extra moisture will make the stems more pliable. This is particularly relevant for sun-bleached stems.*

Filler Flowers

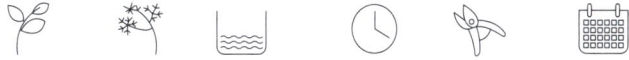

easy to grow • dried • low water • fast growing • CCA • long flowering

filler • heat tolerant • cold tolerant • annual • texture • long vase life

Dried essentials

Pick me	Dry me	Use me
When the flowers are fully open but before seed has developed.	Hang in small bunches upside down to dry (see below).	Massed in a simple ceramic vase or as part of a mixed dried bunch.

Secrets to Dried Bouquets

1 **Hang flowers upside down to dry.**

A dried flower should bear no resemblance to a dead flower. The aim is to retain the shape, form and some of the colour of the fresh stem. To avoid bent, wilted, dead-looking flower heads, stems are suspended upside down using gravity to our advantage.

- Tie small bunches of cut stems with a rubber band. As stems dry, they shrink, so a rubber band works much better than string. Make sure flower heads are not squashed against each other.

- Tip the bunch upside down. This allows plants to dry with straight stems and ensures the petals face upright.

- An easy way of hanging a bunch is to divide it in an upside down 'v' and place it over a long string stretched from wall to wall.

- Drying times vary, so check regularly. Thin stems and fine flower heads dry quickly. Woodier stems and densely petalled flowers take longer.

- Ensure the flower is fully dried before using or storing, to avoid mould and rot.

- An exception to the upside-down rule is rudbeckia. Like hydrangea this dries best upright. The petals fall back towards the stem, revealing a beautiful black central cone.

LEFT If you don't have a dedicated space, improvise. Here, small bunches of statice, winged paper daisy, billy buttons and glossy foliage are tied to an old ladder against a tree. The posy-sized bunches will dry, then be removed before the next rain.

2 Dry the whole bouquet.

Wispy, meadow-style bunches look lovely when dried. Dry each stem individually before combining; a mix of flower shapes works best. Wrap with hessian and tie with a ribbon to complete the effect. Useful flowers include:

Flower	Shape	Colours
Statice	Winged	White, pink, purple, apricot, blue, yellow
Paper daisies	Round	Most except blue
Delphinium and larkspur	Line or spike	White, blue, lavender, pink, purple
Amaranthus	Trailing or plume	Burgundy, green, coral, red
Celosia	Plume, fan, coral	Purple, red, orange, yellow, white, pink, maroon
Sea holly	Thistle	Blue, white
Echinops	Globe	Blue, white
Allium	Globe	Purple, pink, white
Billy buttons	Globe	Yellow
Love-in-a-Mist (*Nigella*)	Texture	Purple to burgundy
Poppy or tulip pods	Texture	Green to biscuit
Kangaroo paw	Airy / texture	Red, mustard, orange, green
Grasses	Line or airy	Biscuit, green

3 Dried wreaths are a long-lasting solution.

Wreaths are not just for Christmas; dried flower versions are lovely any time of the year. That said, they are a great seasonal solution for southern hemisphere gardeners when a hot summer can take a swift toll on a fresh wreath.

Native Australian and South African flowers are especially useful; a wreath can be assembled using fresh flowers and then left to dry. This way both versions can be enjoyed over many months. Fresh and dried stems can also be combined in a wreath. Remember to tightly secure fresh stems to the base as they will shrink when drying.

Dried statice is brilliant for covering wreath bases. Each stem has a number of smaller branches holding the flower 'wings'. These face in different directions making it difficult to handle as a single stem. Snip off the smaller branches before feeding the stem into the wreath base to provide quick and easy coverage. Statice is a generous cut-and-come-again plant so it's easy to build up good reserves for large projects such as this blue and yellow wreath.

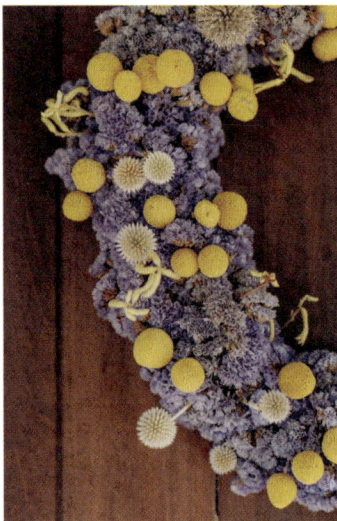

ABOVE Statice, echinops, kangaroo paw and billy buttons hold their colour well for many months when dried.

4 Tips for drying paper daisies.

ABOVE Making a warming winter solstice wreath with dried *Banksia coccinea*, white statice, billy buttons and paper daisies.

Paper daisies make a brilliant dried flower but care needs to be taken with the stems. Thick and tough when the flower is freshly cut, these stems become spindly when dried, especially just below the flower head. As a result, the flowers flop, appearing more dead than dried. These strategies can help:

- When still fresh, snip the flower off the stem and insert a thin wire into the base of the flowerhead. Using these false stems, place the wired flowers upright in a vase.

- Retain the natural stem but use other flowers in the arrangement to support the floppy paper daisy heads.

- Snip off the flower heads and lay flat on a tray to dry. This works well if you're planning to glue the flower heads into a wreath. Make sure there's good airflow, don't overfill the tray.

- Strip the leaves from the stems before drying. Leaves turn an unattractive, wrinkly dark brown when dried.

Foliage

easy to grow • dried • scented • perennial

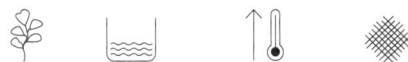

foliage • low water • heat tolerant • texture

Dried essentials

Pick me	Dry me	Use me
Ensure stems are sufficiently mature to retain their shape as they dry.	Hang in small bunches upside down to dry.	In wreaths, foliage bunches or to support and complement other dried flowers.

Secrets of Scented Foliage

1 **Select foliage with a high oil content for fragrance.**

Eucalyptus fits the bill perfectly. A high oil content in leaves, stems and bark give the trees a distinctive fragrance that continues to evolve as the stem dries.

There are hundreds of eucalypt varieties. Blue gum is particularly popular both fresh and dried. Flower Farm favourites include:

- *Eucalyptus cinerea* 'Silver Dollar'
- *Eucalyptus crenulata* 'Victorian Silver Gum'
- *Eucalyptus pulverulenta* 'Baby Blue'
- *Eucalyptus* 'Moon Lagoon'
- 'Spinning Gum' (*Eucalyptus perriniana*)

If you don't have eucalyptus to hand, other high-oil-content foliage works just as well:

- Lavender
- Rosemary
- Sage
- Tea tree
- Myrtle
- Bay
- Lemon verbena
- Cotton lavender

2 **Dry-climate plants dry best.**

Many of the plants that dry best hail from warm climates including Australia, South Africa and the Mediterranean. Adapted to grow in poor soils, plants endemic to these regions have low water requirements and increased drought resilience. As a result, less water is held in stems, leaves and petals, thus requiring a shorter drying time that helps retain natural pigments.

LEFT A full drying barn, with star-shaped alliums and yellow billy buttons, and perfumed by the blue-green eucalyptus leaves.

3 **Many shades of grey.**

One of the challenges associated with drying green foliage is that the fresh, lush leaves tend to become biscuit coloured as they dry out and the chlorophyll degrades. A solution is to dry foliage with silvery-blue, light-toned leaves, rather than deep green leaves.

Flower Farm favourites include:

- Artemesia
- Dusty miller (*Senecio cineraria*)
- Blue gum (*Eucalyptus globulus*)
- Olive (*Olea europaea*)
- Russian sage (*Perovskia*)
- Silver-leafed poplar (*Populus alba*)
- Lamb's ears (*Stachys byzantina*)
- Rose campion (*Lychnis coronaria*)

Use me instead

The purpose of foliage in an arrangement, whether fresh or dry, is to provide a backdrop for the flowers, to support weaker stems and to add volume to the bunch. If dried foliage is not working for you, try using additional airy elements such as grasses or gypsophila. This is particularly effective in meadow-style bouquets.

Blue gum wreath

To form a simple circular wreath, tie several stems of blue gum together, the ends bound by jute string. Select stems that haven't become too woody as these will be more pliable. As the eucalyptus leaves slowly dry, they delicately perfume the air making a delightful wreath for the front door. Or hang in the bathroom and enjoy the fresh, cleansing scent as it's released by steam from the shower or bath. When the wreath is past its best, pop the entire thing onto the compost heap.

RIGHT The round, immature leaves of blue gum eucalyptus.

<u>How to</u>
Press Iceland Poppies

Preserve the ephemeral beauty of dainty Iceland poppies in a flower press or between books to make a decorative candle.

1   With a lit taper candle carefully heat the concave side of a metal spoon. Using the reverse convex side of the spoon, gently press the dried petals to the side of a pillar candle.

2   The heat from the spoon will melt just enough wax to adhere the flower. Don't apply the heated side of spoon to the flower as petals may discolour.

3   Secure all the edges of the flower – this may require reheating the spoon several times.

4   You could use other single-petaled pressed flowers including pansies, cosmos, larkspur, nasturtium, daisies, single dahlias and zinnias.

Airy Elements and Texture

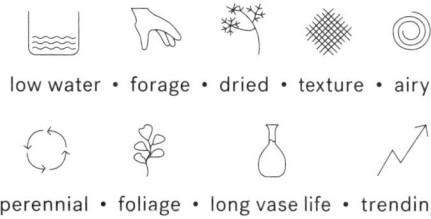

low water • forage • dried • texture • airy

perennial • foliage • long vase life • trending

Dried essentials

Pick me	Dry me	Use me
Forage for cones on branches, seed heads, unusual shapes and textures.	Ensure good airflow. Depending on the item, hang upside down, place in a dry vase or lay on a tray to dry.	To add interest, texture, organic tones and movement.

Ephemeral Secrets

1 **Forage for pods and cones.**

If you've always loved fossicking for seashells and other natural ephemera, you will love creating a textural arrangement with foraged pods, cones and branches. Be conscious of shape and texture. Whether balanced in oversized vases on the branch, wired into wreaths or piled into wide-neck glass vases, dried botanicals in neutral tones are very on trend and bring loads of rugged, attractively coarse texture to a space. Keep your eyes peeled for:

Natives:

- Banksia cones
- Protea stars
- Hakea seed pods
- Gumnuts
- Eucalyptus pods
- Woody pear pods
- Bottle tree seed pods (brachychiton)
- Wattle seed pods

Flower Seed Heads and Pods:

- *Scabiosa stellata*
- Poppy pods
- Sunflower heads
- Baptisia seed pods
- Evening primrose or watsonia seed stalks
- Love-in-a-mist seed pods
- Tulip and lily seed pods
- Echinacea cones without the petals
- Allium seed heads
- Aquilegia seed heads
- Agapanthus seed heads

LEFT Bunny tail and Yorkshire fog grasses are held in bunches using straw napkin rings. The warm biscuit tones are softly highlighted by the addition of *Verticordia densifolia* and stirlingia.

Lanterns:

- Cape gooseberry
- Tomatillo
- Apple of Peru
- Milkweed pods

Other Shapes:

- Cotton stems
- Lotus pods
- Ornamental gourds
- Acorns
- Walnuts
- Rose hips
- Horse chestnuts

2 Pay fresh attention to grasses.

Grasses are the Flower Farm's favourite zero-work ingredient. Wherever you live in the world, there will be grasses to forage. They are usually harvested for drying when a seed head has formed. Many ornamental grasses also have striped or colourful leaves.

Group	Examples
Ornamental garden plants	Pennisetum Panicum Calamagrostis Miscanthus *Chasmanthium latifolium*
Crops / cereal	Triticale Phalaris Wheat Oats Millet
Naturally grown / self sown	Bunny tails Yorkshire fog grass

ABOVE A locally made bud vase is the perfect size for this sweet pea stem.

Handmade pots and vases

Flowers and vase should complement each other. Handmade pots and old earthenware containers work well with many types of flowers. Forage in flea markets and junk shops for vases and unconventional vessels. Or look for the work of local artists in small galleries. The vessels featured in these pages were made by artisans connected to the Flower Farm. While more expensive than mass-produced imports, handmade products are a sustainable choice and support the wider community. Buy fewer, buy better, buy local.

RIGHT Dried 'Drumstick Allium' seed heads and proteas alongside fresh banksias and pendulous gumnuts.

BELOW Hanging aquilegia seed pods and yellow billy buttons to dry.

About
the Authors

Rebecca Starling

I have been fortunate to work for incredible organisations in beautiful places, including the University of Cambridge, the British Foreign Office and a unique school in the Swiss Alps. However, my favourite place has always been the greenhouse. It's where I would rush after work and spend long weekend afternoons. There's something about the smell of damp soil and watching seeds grow into plants that makes me incredibly happy. When I found a way to make a living out of what I loved, there was no looking back. Those stiff suits and pointy shoes were quickly donated to the charity shop, making wardrobe space for dungarees, muddy aprons and other practical gardening garb. I strongly believe that perishable cut flowers should be grown and sold locally. If this book inspires the creation of just a handful of new flower farms or home cutting gardens, it has met its goal. Viva the flower revolution! Discover more about Rebecca and the Flower Farm on Instagram at @starlingflowers_ or at starlingflowers.com.au

Christine McCabe

I have two loves, travel and gardening, and have been documenting my adventures in newspapers and magazines for longer than I care to remember. For a long while it was a peripatetic existence; I once lived in a remote weather station in the high Artic as archivist for a North Pole expedition, filing reports for *The Times* in London. But after putting down roots in the lovely Adelaide Hills, I swiftly fell in love with gardening, a journey detailed in two books, *A Garden in the Hills* and *Adelaide Hills Gardens*. Between travel assignments I spend a lot of time weeding and taking care of a small menagerie. Garden history and the culture of gardening are of abiding interest. Since meeting Rebecca my gardening has improved immeasurably, and I, too, have become addicted to growing dahlias. Find Christine on Instagram at @agardeninthehills or at theoakstradingcompany.com

Index

Bold entries indicate photos.

Acknowledgements

Rebecca would like to thank:

My husband, James, a clever strategist who (ever ahead of his time) had the idea for the Flower Farm a decade before its inception. Thank you for leading the initial infrastructure projects and for dedicating a paddock to the Flower Farm. I appreciate your complete, unwavering support and am quietly impressed by your now-comprehensive flower knowledge.

Christine McCabe, co-author and friend. Always funny, kind and caring. Owner of a very big and very small dog, hordes of chickens and rather scary geese. Constantly and obsessively battling rabbits and mice. Drinker of tea. Writer of beautiful words. This book simply wouldn't have happened without your wisdom, dedication and grit.

Those wonderful people who have worked on the Flower Farm over the years, tackling weeds and pitching in with mass seasonal plantings and other jobs.

My family of inspirational gardeners: my mother, innovative in promoting hardy annuals and organic practices; my father, a considered gardener with a very orderly vegetable patch; my brother, growing drought- and heat-tolerant Mediterranean perennials in pots in his sunny courtyard garden in Aix-en-Provence, France; and my sister with her beautiful hillside garden in snowy Deeside, Scotland, with short seasons and jaw-dropping views.

The people of Robe and Kingston SE, who have shared kind words and encouraged the evolution of the Flower Farm in so many ways.

Christine would like to thank:

Rebecca: friend, fellow dahlia tragic and kindly mentor who never arrives at The Oaks without a car full of gorgeous flowers. Her journey since arriving in Australia has been quite extraordinary, transforming, by sheer force of will (and plenty of detailed planning), a bare cow paddock into the most incredibly productive and beautiful flower farm. She is always generous in sharing her hard-earned knowledge and inspires everyone who visits the farm or attends a workshop. This book is a testament to her passion, vision, great style and tireless work.

My wonderful husband, Melvin, a constant support, and my darling sons, Seb and Kenny, who did so much to help in the garden when they were growing up (if somewhat reluctantly!).

And finally, a big thank you to Georgie Girl and Wee Frank. You know who you are.

We would both like to thank:

Chris Morrison, photographer extraordinaire and worker of magic. His photos are incredible, and even more accomplished given that every shoot seemed to coincide with storms, winds and torrential rain.

Our wonderful team at Thames & Hudson, including editor Sally Holdsworth, designer Emily O'Neill, and the brilliant publishing team, headed by the always-enthusiastic Kirsten Abbott, ably supported by the kindly Lisa Schuurman and Fay Helfenbaum.

The artists and South Australian small businesses who have supplied vases, antiques and clothing featured in the photos: Brioni Pridham, Sophia Legoe, Miss Rose Sister Violet and the shipping container ladies of Workshop 24 in remote Kimba.

First published in Australia in 2024
by Thames & Hudson Australia
Wurundjeri Country,
132A Gwynne Street,
Cremorne, Victoria 3121

First published in the
United Kingdom in 2025
By Thames & Hudson Ltd
181a High Holborn
London WC1V 7QX

First published in the
United States of America in 2025
By Thames & Hudson Inc.
500 Fifth Avenue
New York, New York 10110

Secrets from the Flower Farm

Text © Rebecca Starling and Christine McCabe 2024
Images © Christopher Morrison
christophermorrison.com.au
Images on pages 104 (lilies), 107 (teddy bear sunflower), 112 (digiplexis),
122 (nasturtium), 143 (pink chrysanthemums, top left) and
145 (ikebana) © Rebecca Starling
Photo styling by Rebecca Starling

27 26 25 24   5 4 3 2 1

ISBN 978-1-760-76377-0
ISBN 978-1-760-76484-5 (U.S. edition)

NATIONAL LIBRARY OF AUSTRALIA

A catalogue record for this
book is available from the
National Library of Australia

Front cover: Image by Christopher Morrison,
designed by Emily O'Neill
Design: Emily O'Neill
Editing: Sally Holdsworth
Printed and bound in China
by 1010 Printing International Limited

FSC
MIX
Paper | Supporting
responsible forestry
www.fsc.org   FSC® C016973

Thames & Hudson Australia wishes to acknowledge that
Aboriginal and Torres Strait Islander peoples are the first
storytellers of this nation and the Traditional Custodians
of the land on which we live and work. We acknowledge their
continuing culture and pay respect to Elders past and present.

thamesandhudson.com.au

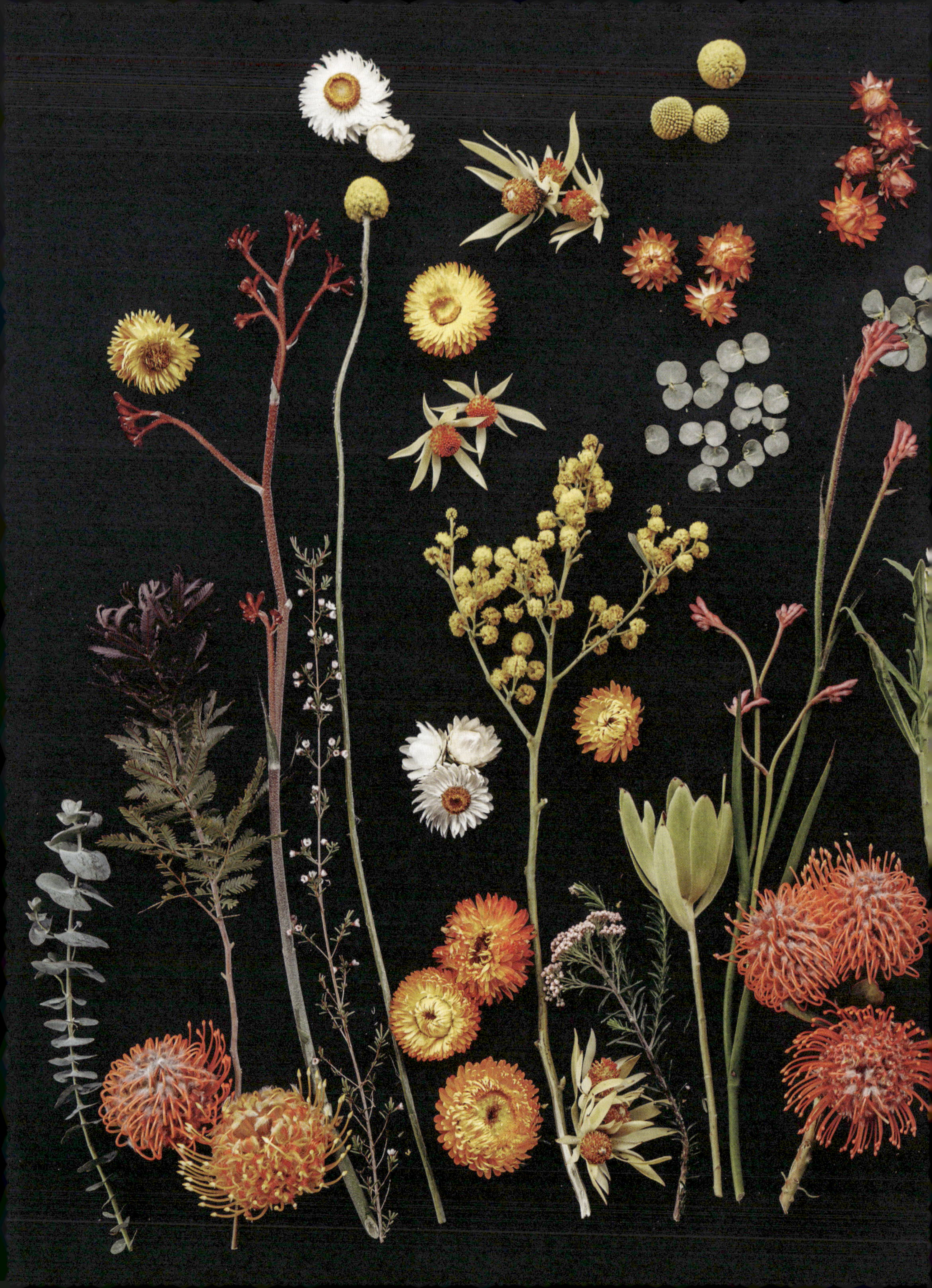